EARTH TO BROCKTON

Jay White

First Edition

Fulton Books, Inc.
Meadville, PA

Published by Fulton Books 2022

ISBN 978-1-63860-952-0 (paperback)
ISBN 978-1-63860-953-7 (digital)

Printed in the United States of America

CONTENTS

PREFACE

One of my goals before turning fifty at the end of May 2021 was to have this compilation of stories sealed together in a way that makes sense so that I can have a manuscript prepared to send to the publisher while I was still in my forties. After that, I didn't know if this would be accepted or not. But I figure the ball will be out of my court, and the decision is no longer up to me—for now. So, technically, I guess I could say I had written a book. Jay White wrote a book! My goodness! Will my obituary say I authored a book? Will this book be the first of more? Will someone famous read it—and laugh? Will my stories be shared? Will only my mother and sister purchase a copy and then the rest only be distributed to Little Free Libraries throughout the city? Will this inspire others to write and share their stories? Who knows?

In 1988, I went to summer school for English. No, nothing fancy to improve my writing and grammatical skills. Simply either go to summer school or repeat a year. I failed English class—miserably—my junior year, and at that time, being at a Catholic high school, all failures needed to be made up if you wanted to return the following autumn. I still don't understand grammar rules. Put a gun to my head, and I still could not tell you what a gerund or a dangling modifier or a past participle is, let alone why they do or don't make sense. In fact, in second grade, when I was absent for a week of school because of a move, I missed out on the introduction of nouns, verbs, and adjectives. So to this day, if you could hear my self-talk, I need to stop and revert to an eight-year-old's thought process and ask myself, "Is this a person, place, or thing?" It does not come naturally!

There are 2.7 million veterans who deployed to Iraq and/or Afghanistan. Each of us has a backstory. We are not just nameless, faceless people who stepped up when the heat came on. Every one of us grew up somewhere. Many of us have siblings. We all went to school. We played sports, and we were in the neighborhood. People know us, and they remember us. Now for those of us who survived, we live on. We use the VA—or not. We go to school or work or stay at home or have no home. We have stories. We don't share them all the time. When we do, rarely do we write those down. Rarer even, if we do tell them and write them down, we don't often share what we have written. So I wanted to capture some of those backstories.

Each story is unique. Mine is unique. I joined the Army Reserves when I was twenty-seven and turned twenty-eight the day basic training began. I was old. I had a college degree, which I could not pay for at the time. What was I to do? I could not find likable, steady work. So instead, I bounced around a ton. In 1996, in fact, I had six jobs in four states and two countries. None of those jobs paid more than about $10 an hour. Those days were a struggle, and I really doubted myself, and sometimes, I didn't think I would ever get out from under all of that.

Everything changed on Tuesday, September 11, 2001. Everything! That infamous day took my trajectory and completely shifted it in another direction. After years of intimate conversations with so many veterans, I have learned that most things we do in life include our thoughts, feelings, emotions, and purpose—but we don't always talk about this. We certainly don't always allow others to know this. These approaches to life go beyond that of combat veterans. I believe what I can share has value for everyone. Some of these stories were fun to think about. Others were not. Sometimes I cringed when I pressed send, as I did not know what the reaction might be. Other times, I had a good, hearty laugh and could not wait to post as I figured many would appreciate my anecdote.

It's 2021 right now. Three hundred years in our future, what will exist from 2021 that anyone will take notice of in 2321? Maybe not much. There definitely won't be much that is not written down, as I imagine it. This book is my attempt to do a few things. Writing the stories that make up this book allows the opportunity to preserve moments that mark our time. Don't go looking it up right away, but off the top of your head, think of something from three hundred years ago—1721! Go ahead. Abe Lincoln? No, he was in the eighteen hundreds. George Washington? Maybe. His big year was 1775–76. Was he even born yet by 1721? Did Abe Lincoln ever meet George Washington? No? Did their lives ever overlap (like a Venn diagram)? A simple Google search will tell you that the future General Washington was not even yet born in 1721. And George and Abe never lived at the same time. So I know nothing for sure about 1721—not without looking it up, that is. Even then, the only things listed (Pope Innocent VIII takes the papal helm, South Carolina becomes a royal territory) are things I had not known about. What is definitely not easily accessible is, What did the everyday commoner do? We can only imagine.

These stories told are real. I do my best to be accurate (quick access to Google and other social media certainly made that easier compared to using the available technology when many stories took place—which is fascinating). I like to think my stories are unique or that I write them with some sort of niche. My niche is threading in a kind of feeling and point to each account. The facts that make up a good story are a strong foundation. But my goal is to allow the reader to feel like they experienced this story. Maybe they read something from me, and that "brought them back" or reminded them of something they experienced.

Perhaps my stories will arouse humor. They may elicit sadness or wonder. That's okay. In fact, I think that is great. We all may have similar feelings, and they may come alive here. I hope they do. I hope you laugh. I expect you to need to put the book down at some point and go cry. Most of all, I hope you connect on some level and at least gain that so many of us have such terrific similarities, which bring you a sense of relief and comfort. I want you to be there, to feel it, to imagine it happening to you, and maybe for the story to enlighten a tale of your own.

The title that I chose for this book is *Earth to Brockton* for a few reasons. Having been born there, it seemed like a natural fit. But it is in Brockton where I always felt most comfortable. Brockton is where my parents met. It is where I started school. It is where all four of my grandparents, five uncles, and four aunts were neighbors. Even after we moved away, we continued to go to Brockton. We were there on all the important holidays and throughout the year, especially in summer. It is where many of my memories began (or happened), and, most importantly, including Brockton in this title is my tribute to give something back to the people there. I have such fond memories and only speak highly of Brockton. But I know the city has struggled for many years.

"It's not what it used to be," I hear people say about it when they are keeping it nice. Gone are the days of Marciano and Hagler. Gone are the tanneries and the shoe factories. Gone even are Purity Supreme and the name of St. Edward's Church. You often hear Brockton mentioned very negatively—the crime, the drugs, the violence. To me though, it is kind of the center of my universe. It is my grandparents' backyard that I imagine whenever I am asked to "close your eyes and think of a safe space." It is where I was most comfortable in life. I will always love Brockton, if only in memory. So the name of this book is a tribute to the love I have for Cary Hill, Mulberry Street, D.W. Field Park, and the City of Champions. May you rise again!

INTRODUCTION

This is not a memoir. This is a group of stories that are not necessarily related. During the isolation that was COVID-19, I had minimal opportunity to do one thing I love to do: tell stories. So I decided to share them in the form of writing. I had almost forgotten how much I enjoyed writing. After I had written and shared a handful of them—and received a positive response—I thought it would be wise to compile the stories. I put them all on my Google docs and then copied and pasted each finished product to the "Stories Shared" folder. Before long, I was up to thirty-three pages of single-spaced, twelve-point-font work. That was much more than anything I had written in either of my master's programs. So I started to wonder how long this would stretch out to in a book. I searched different sites, and I began opening books—all over the place: Barnes & Noble, the Little Free Pantry down the street, anything we had at home, and I would count how many words authors were putting in each line of type, then counted how many lines were on each page. I got the number 330 in my head as to how many words fill a book's page. That's a rough estimate. I looked up how many words serve a novel. I decided to start to aim for fifty thousand words. If I could get fifty thousand words, I ought to contact a publisher and see what I need to do to get my work in print.

To put the stories in some sort of groupings, I chose to take a chronological route. There could be many more stories under each subheading. But that was not the goal here. This was done to keep this compilation easier for the reader to find a story. A beauty of this book is that it does not need to be read from cover to cover. A reader can open it up, find something shorter because they are on a quick bus ride to work, and go for it. Maybe what they read in that short passage puts a smile on their face or changes their attitude or provokes thought or memory.

If you find this and are reading it in 2321, I wish you well, and I hope that you share with others around you. Maybe it will add a little color to a time you may not have thought about. Then please write and share what your life is like. Some folks in 2621 will want to know how it was for you.

Thank you for reading. Enjoy!

SECTION 1

THE RED SOX

There was an old bookstore tucked between the clothing boutiques, mini-art studios displaying goods produced by local artisans, and shanties selling tickets for boat rides and lobster rolls in Perkins Cove. I put down four rolled up one dollar bills to purchase William Jaspersohn's *The Ballpark*. I was eight years old. The Red Sox had already been a big part of my life, and my love for that team only grew more over the years. That same summer, my parents took my sister and me to my first game. The Red Sox defeated Seattle, 7-1, but we had lost our tickets and did not arrive until the bottom of the third inning. I will never forget hearing public address announcer Sherm Feller's voice ringing through the Fens as we walked up to the old yard and then the view we got as we climbed through the tunnel on the third base side. Immediately upon entering Fenway Park, Sox' catcher Carlton Fisk had just doubled, and the legendary Carl Yastrzemski moved to third. Yaz, as they called Captain Carl, wore an iconic helmet that had a pronounced earhole cutout. As soon as I looked down, there it was—that earhole. I had only seen that on TV. Here it was, live. That was the first memory I have in person.

I was hooked…and hooked hard! Sure, like many fans, I tried to watch and listen to every game I could not beg my parents to bring me to, and my mood was almost always in direct alignment with the most recent result or state of the team. When the Boston Red Sox win, Jay is happy and, in fact, sociable and pleasant. If the Red Sox lose? Watch out! I was not the person you would want to be around. I was a grouch! I got close to thinking that my watching the team had some way of affecting the actual result. To know me is to associate me with the Red Sox. In 1998 I was asked to leave my position by a local business I had been working with, editing business cards of all things (it was incredible what my communications degree led me to) for making too many mistakes. I literally jumped in my car and drove directly to Fenway Park. I walked up to the delivery gate on then Yawkey Way and asked the gentleman at the gate if I could meet with Joe Mooney. Not everyone would know who Joe Mooney was then. But if you were a diehard fan like me and a lover of neatly mown grass and the beauty of a major league ballpark, you paid enough attention to know that Mr. Mooney was the keeper of the ground sat the place I considered the center of my universe.

I think the gate guard was impressed with my conviction and, thus, was allowed to go inside the empty but hallowed ballpark on this early Spring weekday morning. I met Joe in the lower box seats behind the third base dugout as he was coming in off the field.

"What do you want?" Joe barked out to me. I told Joe Mooney I would offer him my services. Without hesitation, he said, "Where do you live?" Where do I live? Really? Are you kidding me? He didn't say no! In fact, Joe asking me where I live was in line with the feeling I got when the answer my dad might give me when I did ask to go to Red Sox games as a child, and the request was not being declined. This could be good! I was immediately stoked!

"Dorchester," I told him. At the time, I was renting out a room in a third floor bedroom in a triple-decker behind the Dunkin' Donuts near Everett Square.

"When can you start?" Joe continued. When can I start? For real? Oh my goodness! Forget my bachelor's degree. Forget my future plans. All I knew was in two hours, I was mercifully released from a mindless job in a windowless office with a nonsocial work crew to an opportunity to work outside and needing to pinch myself at that moment at—no—on Fenway Park! On Fenway Park. I would have told Mr. Mooney I could start that day, but I didn't want to appear too over eager. So I told him I could begin "tomorrow." He gave me two days, and I was there bright and early, pulling off the wet tarp that Friday morning—the weekend before opening day! For the only time in my adult life, the night before my first day of employment at Fenway Park, I could hardly sleep as I was so excited to go to work the next day.

It was quite a thing to crest the boundary that was the walls at a major league facility. The days of innocently taking a seat next to my father deep in the right field grandstands, getting to the park early to watch batting practice, eating a hot dog, and rooting on the likes of Dewey, Lynn, and Rice were forever changed once you exposed yourself to the under workings of the day-to-day rigors of working for and watching Major League Baseball. It was a great experience to manicure the bullpen mounds, rake the infield and sit with Red Sox relievers during games. I got to rub shoulders with big-league ballplayers. I got to sit in the visitors' dugout and have an hour-long conversation with the then Yankees coach, Don Zimmer, and reminisce about the illustrious late 1970s team of my youth. But when it was all said and done, nothing beat the excitement of heading in on Storrow Drive with Dad, wondering where we would park, if we could still get a couple of tickets for that night's game, and thinking that this might be the start of the rally that puts the Red Sox over the top.

YOU MAKE THE CALL

One afternoon in a game with the Cleveland Indians when I was the right field ball "boy" at Fenway Park, Red Sox catcher Jason Varitek hit a soft looping ball over the Tribe's first baseman, Jim Thome, who was twisting back to track the ball. The ball landed beyond Thome and directly on the foul line, making a distinct thud sound. The first base umpire had much difficulty seeing past Thome's wide-set shoulders, and I noticed that he had at least some uncertainty. Naturally (after all, I am a fan first), I confidently indicated that the ball was fair. The ump seemed to look right at me…and copied my gesture. (It's okay. Replay wasn't around then, but it would have proven I was correct.)

MO VAUGHN NIGHT

In the last weeks that Mo Vaughn was still with the Red Sox, he hosted his final Mo Vaughn Night event at the Sheraton Hotel in Boston's Back Bay. It was cool because Mo, who had a big bat and a bigger heart, would raise money for kids all over the city. He would invite many folks—the Fenway Park grounds crew, of which I was a member in 1998, Red Sox teammates and office personnel, and even other Boston athletes and celebrities—to attend this wonderful dinner and auction right around Christmastime.

Red Sox radio announcer Joe Castiglione, whose voice had been as much a part of my youth as my own parents', was emceeing the after-dinner live auction. I was barely paying any attention to the fundraising goings-on as the item's minimum bids would have bankrupted my measly savings—then anyway. After milling about and having taken pictures next to the stunning Christmas tree and with Mo himself, I noticed the then-Sox batboy sitting at a table up toward the front of the room. The bat boy was just below the podium from which Castiglione was hawking big-ticket items that would certainly help meet financial goals for the annual event. Being friendly and having noticed a familiar face, I raised my hand to gesture "hello." I don't think the batboy ever even saw me. But Castiglione did. "You. $600!" the man now famous for his "can you believe it?" catchphrase that debuted the night the Sox later broke the curse in '04 announced to the bidders as he pointed right at me.

What? Six hundred dollars! For what? Me? Holy cow! No way. Joe Castiglione had me pinned as the newest high bidder and potential owner of one pair of white game-used John Elway cleats. John Elway! The Denver Broncos' quarterback famous for "The Drive!" Not even a Patriot! I don't even like the Broncos. *Why would John*

Elway's cleats even be at this auction? was one of the many thoughts that flashed through my mind in this nano-second that seemed to be ten minutes long suddenly. Regardless, the long-toothed, rifle-armed QB's old shoes are about to be all mine—albeit for two to three weeks of my pay, unless someone outbids me here quickly! With a few hundred people in attendance, the silence began to deafen me (although I started hearing my heartbeat).

Celtics' legend Cedric Maxwell, seated at the table next to mine, was losing his mind in laughter as he picked right up on what was unfolding. When he could open his eyes, as they crinkled closed in disbelief and in reaction to what he thought was pure comedy, he was staring right at me (with tears welling on the bottom lids). His wicked long fingers covered his wide-open mouth as he could not get enough of this. He looked to be using his gala chair as a balancing tool as his what-appeared-to-be-seven-foot-long-body was pointing in a perfectly straight forty-five-degree angle like a clock hand pointing at the ten.

I could not let old Cornbread distract me at this moment. If I did not alert Castiglione that he and I had simultaneously come to a huge misunderstanding, I would be in a bad spot financially (well, let's be more accurate: a worse place). I saw a future of poverty ahead of me. If I did not rise up and correct this action, my appeal could not wait another second. I desperately flung both arms back and forth up in the air for all to see. Be no mistaking my now-desperate plea. I do not want John Elway's cleats! I cannot have John Elway's cleats even if I did want them. I hope to have a family one day. These cleats threatened my future children's chance to exist if I don't get out from under this potential purge of having to fork over all that I own for a pair of John Elway's cleats that he probably wore for one half against the San Diego Chargers.

Thankfully, somehow, Castiglione did see my resistance, but of course not without a little more embarrassment of him loudly questioning my rebuttal to confirm denial of the bid! Then the good-natured Maxwell only increased his laughter/crying and looked like he would need to gain control of himself soon or he might be in trouble. Instead, Maxwell couldn't help himself but reenact how I looked, trying to say "No!" Seeing his now-outstretched arms (as he was showing me what I had just looked like) up so close left me with no doubt how he used to be able to slam-dunk the rock back in his day. In the moment of relief, I was suddenly off the hook for $600 that I didn't have. The show had moved on. Then I recognized how much I appreciated Cedric Maxwell and his ability never to lose sight of what is most important—that we all make mistakes, and sometimes we just need to lighten up a little and laugh at ourselves.

NICE GAME FOR A DAY

It was a beautiful spring morning, the long-awaited date of the Red Sox home opener in 1998. It was the first game I would work as a member of the Fenway Park ground crew. The Sox were hosting the Seattle Mariners. I was on the field several hours before game time, by myself at one point, when I was walking from the third-base dugout to the left-field corner. I would then make my first interaction with a ballplayer when the two of us were there to "do our job."

Seattle closer Bobby Ayala was also alone. He was sitting on the grass in foul territory, starting to stretch. Not saying something to him would have been stranger than greeting him. As I got as close as I would, a wave of nervousness came over me. I did not just say hello to him like I probably would have if he were a "person on the street" who was too close not to say something. Instead, I bobbled my first try. "Nice game for a day, huh?" I muttered. (Self-talk began immediately: Really, Jay? Seriously? That is what you come up with?)

He nodded and said, "Yup!" I always wondered if he just thought I was a funny smart-ass.

RICO BROGNA'S HOME RUN

August 2000, Fenway Park

I had heard that Rico Brogna, who had come over to the Red Sox from Philadelphia following a very productive offensive year for him, grew up as a Red Sox fan. I recall hearing stories of him connecting with older relatives and running around celebrating in the North End when he was a kid, following Sox wins. So I thought it must be so great for him to live out the dream that many New England kids have: suiting up and playing for the Boston Red Sox. Then imagine getting to do that and even hitting a home run for the Olde Towne Team? That's almost too good to be true.

Well, Rico got to live that out. And I won't forget it!

In a game with the then-Tampa Bay Devil Rays, Rico hit a game-winning home run, a grand slam nonetheless. The evening was a damp one, and the weather was unstable. It was the kind of later-summer night that seemed like a shower was on the radar, and the pre-rain event appeared in the form of a steady misty scenario. As he circled the bases and the hearty remaining fans celebrated to The Standells en route to the exits, I sprinted out to cover the bullpen mounds, which I knew would save me a ton of work the next day if I could keep those as dry as possible. Though the horse was essentially out of the stable for me accomplishing that goal, I hustled out anyway. When I opened the Devil Rays' bullpen door, there rested the now-slick Brogna home run ball. I put the ball in my pocket, sprinted over to the Boston bullpen, covered those mounds and then made my way back into the Red Sox dugout.

Rico was standing in front of the Boston dugout, preparing to do a postgame TV interview. I bumped him in the shoulder and presented him with the ball. He was very grateful, and I could feel how he must have felt, having had such a tremendous real-life experience. That was the only home run Rico would hit with the Red Sox. I am so pleased that he got the ball back. If only he knew the guy giving it to him was as big a fan as he had been, I think he would appreciate that ball even more.

TRACTOR VERSUS OUTFIELD WALL

I was on the tractor, dragging the warning track at Fenway Park, preparing to get the field in top shape for that afternoon's game against the Yankees. I turned around in the deep right field and headed back toward center, but in a path closest to the wall. New York catcher Joe Girardi was a few feet away, on the grass with a coach to my left. I was impressed by a workout routine Girardi was doing—working on blocking pitches while utilizing something other than a typical mitt—and kind of got caught up watching him.

SHHHRRIPPPPP! *Uh-oh, what the hell was that?* I thought after having heard this most unusual but also unwanted sound. I looked down behind me and saw that I had just clipped the bottom corner of one of the sections of outfield padding, up against the visitors' bullpen, with the back of the tractor. I ripped it up pretty well. The green-painted vinyl outer portion flipped back and up, completely exposing the subdermal plywood and black foam pad. The plywood was cracked but not separated and now hanging upside down and looking like a giant slice of pizza. A gaffe like this may not have been a huge deal if I was in my backyard, but it was not the case at Fenway Park, as thousands of fans and a national television audience had been due to arrive and tune in very shortly.

I quickly parked the tractor in front of the mishap, blocking the site of the tear from everyone. Knowing that any abrupt or unusual activity on my behalf would potentially raise eyebrows and undoubtedly draw negative attention, I hopped off the then-parked tractor. I faked that I needed to get something in the adjacent bullpen. I did a BS walk in there, acted like I was checking something else out and then circled back. Doing this bought me time and provided me the chance to assess the damage and make a cut-rate plan on rectifying the issue without asking for help and jeopardizing the game—or my reputation. (It was necessary on the grounds crew to minimize gaffes, or else you risked being cannon fodder for the remainder of the summer).

Next, I thought of myself as looking like Rowan Atkinson doing one of his goofy Mr. Bean roles: recognizing the magnitude of the error, the small amount of time to do something about it, being solely responsible for the mistake, and not wanting any attention—a terrible mix! Also, like Bean, I think I may have nonverbally hummed and made smirking sounds as I Mickey-Moused that pad's corner back into decent shape with a shove here and a fold-under and tuck there. Step back, take a look. Not bad! I wouldn't punch it to test it, but no one noticed. The area did not appear unsafe. It probably could have used a couple of reinforcement staples on the backside, but that would need to wait until next off-season. If ever I personified the feeling of the interjection "whew," it was as I drove that tractor back under the left-field grandstands and went about my day.

YEAH! I SAW HIM DO THAT

Several hours before a night game against the Red Sox, New York Mets reliever Turk Wendell placed a baseball on the lip of the outfield grass directly behind where the shortstop would stand, at Fenway Park. He took off his right shoe and two-stepped up to the ball. Turk kicked it into the screen (which has since been replaced with seats) over the Green Monster.

PEDRO'S ILLUS

I had just gotten done manicuring the Red Sox bullpen mounds and cutting the grass one slow weekday morning when Pedro Martinez, for whatever reason, came out to throw a side session. The Sox' pitching and bullpen coaches accompanied him. Jason Varitek was there to perform the catching duties. I recognized this as a great chance to do something any baseball fan would want to do if they had gotten the opportunity that was suddenly sitting on my proverbial plate. So I strategically sat on the bullpen bench—positioned thirty feet from Pedro and thirty feet from Tek—or right in the middle. The bench itself was less than ten feet away from the path of the pitch. The view I had of the then-most dominant pitcher in the world, and now Hall of Famer, was priceless.

I try to remain honest and reduce exaggeration to sustain the value of my perspective, especially when I write and share a story with a broader audience. But when Pedro Martinez ripped off some of his moneymaking sliders that day, from my vantage point, the ball gave the illusion of completely stopping its spin only to then pick up a new rotation and absolutely dart into the left-handed batters' box. I had and have seen many a baseball pitch thrown. I have NEVER seen that before.

UMPIRE VERSUS MANAGER

Everyone in Major League Baseball knows that the Sunday before the July All-Star Game is a mass exodus when that day's game concludes. Unless a player, coach, or umpire is involved in the Summer Classic, this is the only collective break in the grueling 162-game season, and most of these men are eager to go home and get a quick visit in with their children, wives, and families—a chance to sleep in their bed, many say. In 1998, the Chicago White Sox were visiting Boston on this annual "getaway day." I was the Red Sox's right field ball boy (that term should have been used loosely; I had just turned twenty-seven years old), down past first base and the tarp at Fenway Park. In the top of the fifth inning, the phone rang in "Canvas Alley." "Jay! When this inning is over, go out and tell the first base umpire that there has been a change in his flight, and he needs to get with the travel secretary immediately after the game ends!" I was ordered.

Well, a couple of batters later, the Chicago side of the inning ends on a bang-bang play at first base. I do as they told me and head over to the ump, but so does the South Siders' manager. This was before instant replay, and White Sox manager appeared to need to tell the umpire that from his vantage point, some 150 feet away, his view of the play was more accurate. The skipper comes storming out of the visitor dugout and rips across the infield en route to first base—the umpire. Suddenly, I found myself in the most awkward of positions: on the field and in clear sight of everyone, waiting in line to talk to an umpire who was going to town on a manager. I mean, they were going at it! Classic nose-to-nose. Screaming! Spitting! Neck veins popping out of both men. I am just a few feet away, trying to give them respectable space! The man in blue finally has it with Chicago's field boss and tosses him from the game. Eventually, he said his peace and departs. Immediately after that, the ump, who knew I was there, turns to me and, as calm as a dad might say to one of his kids on a lazy summer day while standing in the driveway, says, "What can I do for you?"

So I guess I told him what needed to be said, but I was frozen not by his words but by his demeanor. *Wait? What? You're not bothered by that argument that you had (three seconds ago)?* I thought with my mouth agape, probably looking like *A Christmas Story's* Ralphie looked when his Orphan Annie secret decoder reminded him to drink Ovaltine. I learned more about professional baseball in that one minute than I had in years of watching it on TV. I haven't looked at it the same since…, and I still love it!

RICE, LYNN, EVANS, MANNY (AND ME?)

As a little kid, I really couldn't imagine not being a Major League Baseball player one day. I heard about the odds and the competition, but that never registered early on. We would go to see the Red Sox at Fenway Park. We got there early. We bought tickets at the gate and watched all of the batting practice. I marveled at the distance, speed, accuracy, and "frozen rope" trajectory of the tosses that outfielders Jim Rice, Dwight Evans, and Fred Lynn would make with grace and ease to each other. *That would be me one day*, I thought. So, I worked on that. My friend Matt, especially, was my go-to partner daily.

Time marched on—reality set in. I didn't even come close. I was marginal at best. However, one night, when I worked for the Red Sox and was in the home bullpen during a game ("in case a ground crew member needed to retrieve an on-field beach ball, more than anything"), left fielder Manny Ramirez got my attention during a Sox pitching change. For some reason, he wanted a ball. Well, the relievers' bucket-o-balls was right beside me. Without thinking much, I grabbed one. Then, as I looked at him, it was 1979 all over again. I have one chance to do what Lynn and Rice and Evans did. Though I could never hit well and have no speed, I always had a pretty decent arm. I fired that ball to Manny. I hit him in the chest, and he didn't have to move. I was in deep center. He was in the left field corner. Wow! I always thought, *I hope some eight-year-old kid saw that and thought, Cool! Did you see that guy throw that ball that far?*

NO RUNS, NO DRIPS, NO ERRORS

It was a nationally televised Saturday afternoon game at Fenway Park in the late 2000 season with the Yankees in town. The home plate umpire claimed that the dry conditions of the red clay were causing home plate to blend in too much with the color of the batters' boxes. No problem. Hit up the plate with some white spray paint in between innings, and we're all good.

Yours truly was given the honors to go out to the plate as soon as New York lefty Andy Pettitte was done warming up. But here's how that went down for me. Once we heard from Culbreth, I had to quickly vacate the ground crew pit in short right field and head underneath the grandstands, past hundreds of fans in line for concessions, as I could not just cut across the field while the Yankees were batting. I grabbed two cans of white Krylon spray paint from the ground crew's work area, located beside the visitor's clubhouse, behind third base, in the bowels of the old ballyard. Cans in hand, I cut through the Yankees' locker room, down the old flight of stairs into the tunnel and up into the Yankees' dugout. I stood one step below the dugout level because if America didn't need to see anything in the New York Yankees' bench area, it was a Boston employee holding a can of spray paint in either hand.

The Yankees were still batting, so I had to wait. I remember Roger Clemens, a favorite when he was with the Sox but now a Yankee, standing beside me and looking at me skeptically with a face that said, "What in the hell are you doing with those?" Then I was starting to realize I had too much time to start thinking about how this seemingly simple task could go wrong: "What if a nozzle busts? What if I can't get the cap off the can? What if I make a goddamn mess and spray 'outside the lines'? What if a gust of wind catches the mist of paint, and the national camera records me making a buffoon of myself?"

Finally, the New York side was retired. Andy Pettitte strolled to the mound to take his warranted warm-up pitches. I walked out and stood awkwardly in the third base fungo circle, exchanged brief pleasantries with Culbreth, and waited on Pettitte. Eventually, catcher Jorge Posada threw the ball down to second to get the next inning underway. Instead of "Let's have a batter," Culbreth yelled out, "Jorge, hold up!" Posada looked over at me, saw what I was there to do, politely nodded at me, and respectfully backed up, giving me full reign of the area. At this time, I started thinking there are people at a small bar in Guthrie, Oklahoma, and people at a camp in Sweden, Maine, watching this game on TV. There are tons more in their Bronx apartments and probably some dudes joking and laughing in a barbershop in South Carolina also tuning in. I have just been summoned to center stage. The scheduled batter, the catcher, and the umpire are all just standing there, waiting for me, watching! There was plenty of good game left to be played, but not until I made it so people could see home plate. Thank God *Old School* had not yet come out in theaters because I would have gotten more nervous comparing the next moment to when Will Ferrell's character, "Frank the Tank," is nailed in the neck with that tranquilizer dart in the pool scene.

I went to the catcher's side of the plate, took a knee, and BRUSHED THE PLATE OFF. Time suddenly stood still. In my memory, it's like I have a 360-degree view of the whole thing, and it replays in my mind much like a movie would. Next, I SHAKE one of the cans, as is the norm for a can of spray paint. CLINK. DUP. CLINK. DUP. That ball thing inside the can slowly rattled to and fro, but at a pace so slow, I barely recognized the timing of the sound. However, the metal-on-metal-inside-the-can reverberation is refreshingly familiar. Home plate is only seventeen inches across (thus seventeen inches from the front edge to the back point, and by the way, it's tough to see if the edges ar—or were—actually black), but it felt like it was three feet wide, and it seemed like the stream of paint was making a row only about an inch wide. I feel like I made about fifty crossover strokes—from side to side and front to back. I sprayed until the red nozzle's ridges were imprinted into the tip of my index finger.

Thankfully, the air was still, and nothing sprayed haphazardly. The nozzle did not break off. I had gotten the cap off without even thinking about it. And when I was done, Culbreth even said, "Looks good! Thank you!" That was it. Posada walked back up, pulled down his mask, and got in his crouch. Pettitte toed the rubber. The Red Sox's batter kicked fresh dust onto the wet paint, and I went back into the Yankees' dugout and disappeared forever.

THOSE OUTFIELD FOUL LINES

The foul lines beyond the grass in the warning track up to the respective foul poles were made of wood two-by-fours, covered in recycled rubber fire hose, tacked down by roofing nails, painted white, and embedded into the dirt.

SECTION 2

BASEBALL

The one constant through all the years, Ray, has been baseball. America has rolled by like an army of steamrollers. It has been erased like a blackboard, rebuilt, and erased again. But baseball has marked the time.
—James Earl Jones as Terence Mann, *Field of Dreams*, 1989

I recently read a post from a friend that stated something about the feeling a kid gets when he finds the proper grip on a baseball; how comforting and natural that is, and how he grows to love the game. The post concludes by shifting focus from the kid to the sport and suggests that the whole time "It was the other way around." Baseball had its grip on the kid. That was me. Some weekday summer nights, when I was about four or five years old, my mother, sister, and I would sit in the warm grass at Tukis Park in Brockton and watch my father and uncles' softball games. Some of the guys on that team wore metal spikes. When they walked on the concrete near where we were sitting, I heard what I thought was the most incredible sound. Spikes! So cool! So cool to me, in fact, that I found that stepping on an empty tonic (soda) can and walking around on asphalt made a similar, joyous noise. Then when Dad was at work, and I would find his double knit white softball pants in the laundry pile, I would put them on. The pants were twenty sizes too big, but they got me hooked. I wanted to be a ballplayer—like Dad!

I love baseball. People who know me associate me with baseball. I can't walk through the halls at work without a "Hey, you playing this year?" or "Your Sox are looking good." That is me at age fifty. Fifty! Who plays baseball until they are fifty? Outside of only a handful of guys who got paid to do so (Satchel Paige and Julio Franco jump into my mind immediately, but I would need to fact-check myself)? In reality, I stopped playing two years ago when non-baseball injuries led to shoulder woes. I could no longer command pitch location, which became too many walks, then losses, and then me letting it get to my head. I was forty-eight years old, and I started to become too nervous about taking the mound. I had to hang it up. The sport I loved told me so! Baseball is a beautiful teacher. It is the most fantastic game. The bases are the perfect distance from each other. The game has so well reflected our society for over one hundred years. Baseball may appear boring to many, but once the time is taken to patiently discern the pitch-by-pitch strategy happening, it brings on a new world of appreciation. Baseball, like life, gives and taketh away. It is perfect.

My great uncle who died some twenty-three years before I was born and in the same season the world lost Babe Ruth, had covered the Boston Braves for the Globe. He was in his heyday at the time of Shoeless Joe Jackson and provided written suspicions of the effects upon the Black Sox scandal. His niece, my grandmother, followed "Uncle Jim" to many Red Sox game at Fenway Park when Jim had become the official scorer of now Boston's lone hardball franchise. As we called her, Mimi used to tell me how she so loved to especially follow Jimmie Foxx.

"He had the most beautiful eyes," my grandmother told me. When she was a child, Mimi had the fortune of getting to sit in the box seats behind the Sox dugout, allowing her incredible close-up views of the game and its players in a time when most can only dream about it.

Later, my father introduced me to the same Globe's daily American League standings in 1978. It was less of an educational moment and more like an immediate start of a lifelong relationship that was meant to be. I fell in love, and I have not let go. Baseball has been the most consistent part of my life. Through childhood moves, life events, school, work, becoming a parent, a husband, a homeowner, a soldier, a federal employee, the only thing that remains constant in my life has been baseball, Fenway Park, and the Red Sox. That part has always been there. I can find a YouTube video of the Sox dropping a home game to the Oakland A's the afternoon I was born, and I am tired today writing this as I was up late watching the Sox championship game versus Houston last night—from the exact location in the Back Bay. I loved playing ball. I could not hit, and I didn't run fast. But I always had a good arm, and I developed a love for pitching. Ultimately, I did not throw hard enoug, and I was reminded of that when I was cut from my college's team four times in four years of trying out. I kept playing, though. I enjoyed many a competitive night in Boston's Yawkey League, hurling for the Savin Hill Hornets, and I got selected to pitch once at Fenway in a league all-star game. What a thrill. Baseball is my comfort zone. For some years, I thought it was about time to grow up and move away from that. Shortly after, and instead, I chose to dismiss that thought and embrace it. I love baseball and always will. Why give something up that is so important to me?

TALKING TO DONNIE BASEBALL

I walked into the quiet Yankees locker room at the old Yankee Stadium on Mother's Day morning, just a few months before the infamous players' strike led to the first season without a World Series in ninety years. I felt like I shouldn't be there. After all, I am one of the biggest Boston Red Sox fans that I have ever known, and I often wonder if my love for the Olde Towne Team matches my disdain for their rivals—and the owners of this sacred space, the New York Yankees. It's a pretty relative measure. Plus, for all the Yankees fans that care so much about their team, it seemed unfair that I was there, and they have never had this opportunity.

Jim Abbott, famous for being born with only one hand, and a pitcher for the Yanks then who had just twirled a no-hitter a little less than a year earlier, sat alone at a table in the middle of the main section of the room, signing boxes of baseballs. Gerald Williams, an outfielder who got on the radar a few years later when he was with Tampa Bay, challenged Sox ace Pedro Martinez to a fistfight, impressed with his shirtless physique. An older coach, for some reason needing a public shower at this earlyish hour, walked around with his barrel chest tucked into a bland towel. My only self-constructed rule there was to keep moving—and not be asked to leave. I had credentials, as I was there for my new joint undertaking as producer and co-host, along with my buddy Mike St. Hilaire of WZNN's new sports program, "Obstructed View." We were there to "work." Yeah, right. Back then, and even still, I did not think having fun and loving what I did was work. Oh, how far I have to go.

In 1994, the Yankees were a phenomenal team. Some say they were locks for the World Series. But we will never know. At the time, I had no idea there would be no healthy conclusion to that season. I was there to gather whatever tidbits I could collect for the Sox fans back in our show's broadcast range. Talking to these Yankees would qualify as worthy tidbits. But getting good sound bites, especially when I had zero relationships with any player there, and no one even recognized my mug, was not so easy. Then though, the best of all of them welcomed me to his luxurious corner locker space and began talking with me as if he was the one wanting to spark the conversation. It was Don Mattingly. "Donnie Baseball," the Yankees' captain, and onetime MVP and perennial all-star. He, one of the purest hitters of the previous decade and en route to his first play-off season, allowed me to hang out with him for at least fifteen to twenty minutes. With his small speakers producing favorite country music and his sharp cowboy boots pushed to the side, we talked baseball. We talked specifics about the preparation he was doing for that day's game. He impressed me with his knowledge of Boston's Joe Hesketh, the starting pitcher he was ready to face in a few hours. He talked about traveling to Sunapee, New Hampshire, with his wife, in years prior. He was polite. He was friendly. He made me feel like I belonged there. It was pretty cool, I must say.

Don Mattingly is sixty years old today. He has become a pretty remarkable manager. If Mattingly never gets voted into the Hall of Fame, his name will always be on the lips of knowledgeable baseball fans who think he is at least close to receiving a Cooperstown nod. But the greatest of all things with Don Mattingly is that he is just a dude. He showed me that no matter how successful you may be or how accomplished you are, we are all just people, making our way in this world. Some play for the Yankees, some teach, some can't find work, some drive trucks, some don't make adulthood. Regardless, it's all in how we treat each other. Don Mattingly is a champ in my book even if he was a Yankee.

TRIPP CROMER, NO! DAVID WRIGHT, YES!

When the Major League Baseball players' strike ended in 1995, the season opener was pushed back a few weeks to the end of April. I was living in Jersey City at that time. I decided to head out to Shea Stadium as the Mets offered plea-bargain-price tickets—one dollar—to faux-apologize to fans for swiping the end of the previous season away. It was a Sunday morning, and I thought that, despite my disdain for the continuing presence of what seemed like greed to the average fan, it would be really cool to watch the St. Louis Cardinals and Ozzie Smith. "The Wizard of Oz," arguably the greatest defensive shortstop that the game has ever produced—albeit in the sunset of his career—was in town to take on the Mets.

When I got to Manhattan, I took the famous "7 train" to Flushing. For those unfamiliar with the Mets or Flushing, Queens, "the Seven" is such a household term it is probably mentioned more often than Tom Seaver, La Guardia, Arthur Ashe, and the world's fair combined. Then, once at Shea, I hopped in line to get a ticket. I had a small plan to show my dissatisfaction to the powers-that-be for their incongruent relationship with We the Fans. I paid for my upper deck seat with four quarters. That's right. No crisp dollar bill that they were probably expecting from this guy! I would have used ten dimes if I had had them, to spite. (Yeah! I was none too pleased about that strike, and the only "voice" I had was my use of coinage. There was no boycotting here; I loved the game too much. Not following baseball—and that certainly included attending games—would have only hurt me, I thought then.)

Regardless, this is where my little story happens. So I get all the way over to east Queens, ready to watch baseball but mainly excited to lay eyes on this Hall-of-Famer-to-be, who I watched win the 1982

World Series (and his team probably should have won again in 1985 thanks to a blatantly wrong call by Don Denkinger, that was not to be), who did backflips on the field en route to his position on Opening Days in St. Louis, who once made the most remarkable diving play when he was with the San Diego Padres and who taught me fielding skills when he visited Johnny Bench's TV program, *The Baseball Bunch*, one Saturday morning in my youth. I spent a good hour and a half walking and trains and transfers and waiting on platforms (in the pre-iPhone days, we had no choice but to somehow acknowledge each other or prove we were outwardly ignoring each other). I finally climbed into my seat just up under where the Delta and American Airlines' passengers sat when they shook Shea upon takeoff from next door LaGuardia Airport. I glanced out at the iconic right-centerfield scoreboard to see the starting lineups. The lineups, listed vertically there in between the multiple repeat "RC" (cola) signs, just lit up each team's positions with a corresponding uniform number. Many fans—like me then—usually had a pretty good grasp of the number-to-player translation built into their minds. Outside of your favorite team, there were a handful of stars whose uniform numbers were pretty common knowledge. It was widely known that Ozzie Smith wore number one. On the scoreboard under St. Louis, it appeared like this for a starting shortstop: SS-7! What? Why does his one look like a seven? *That has to be a one!* I thought. *Why is there a seven up there?* Being there alone and not one to spark small talk upon being new to a location, I was left to my own auspices.

Lo and behold, enter Tripp Cromer. Who is Tripp Cromer? I had never even heard of Tripp Cromer. Tripp Cromer, who had only a dozen or so major league games under his belt up to that day, was the St. Louis Cardinals' starting shortstop. Tripp Cromer! Not Ozzie Smith. Yup! And Tripp Cromer played the entire game. Ozzie never made an appearance. I'm not sure if Ozzie was even in the building that day. Baseball historians are familiar with the name Wally Pipp. Wally, as it turns out, was kind of the opposite of Tripp Cromer. Across town and many decades prior, those attending a Yankees game would have shown up to see Pipp out of the starting lineup one day but replaced with the legend of legends, Lou Gehrig. Gehrig never returned that spot to Pipp. Not here. Now I got Pipp Cromer. I wanted to see the Wizard. Even outside the lines, baseball still teaches us about life. The New York Mets organization and Major League Baseball were not responsible for returning me those four quarters—because that is just how life goes.

So it's not all bad though. Because if you keep your eyes open, pleasant surprises you may not expect to see can reveal themselves to you as well. In fact, the New York Mets, who robbed my 1986 Red Sox of a curse-busting World Series, have provided me plenty of payback. The team once issued me a dozen tickets to bring local veterans to see a late-season game from the third base boxes, and R. A. Dickey knuckle-balled his way to a twentieth win that day. The Wounded Warrior Project once asked for veterans to be present for Opening Day at the new Citi Field. I got to bring my father-in-law, a big Metropolitans fan, onto the infield for the national anthem. But most memorable of all is when, in August 2005, my wife and I honeymooned in San Diego. We attended a Mets-Padres game at Petco Park. Old friend Pedro Martinez started that night for the visiting Mets, and the place—strangely—was chock-full of Red Sox fans. However, the highlight was when the Mets' third baseman, David Wright, made an over-the-shoulder barehanded grab of a looping liner. That play, as I proclaimed immediately to my new bride, would be (and has been) on several "Top Plays" lists that I would (and have) come across. We saw it. We did not miss that. Keep your eyes open. You may see great things happen.

LAYOVER WITH BONDS AND SOSA

I got into O'Hare Airport around noon, Central time, one day at the end of July and learned that my layover flight to Boston was delayed—and would leave me in Chicago for about five hours. It was 2003, and I was fresh home from Iraq, so I really didn't care too much about having to wait. It was nice just to be there (or anywhere this side of the Atlantic). To bide my time, I picked up a package of Raisinets and a copy of the *Chicago Sun-Times* at the Hudson News market and then went and took a seat overlooking the tarmac—away from others. Of course, when I opened the paper, I skipped right to the sports pages and, specifically, the baseball updates. Lo and behold, the San Francisco Giants were visiting the Cubs for a getaway game in less than an hour on the North Side.

I immediately shot out of my seat, walked to the ground terminal, and reviewed the Chicago transportation map. The train, or the "L," as they call it there, goes to O'Hare. Holy cow, as the late Harry Caray would say! I was on the next train out, headed to the ball game. The Blue Line brought me right to Addison Street. I got off the train there and transferred to a bus that ran directly to Wrigley Field. For ten bucks, I was in! I got there in the first inning and stayed through the sixth.

Though steroids would bite them both quite hard, at that time, getting to see Sammy Sosa and Barry Bonds was considered quite a treat. My favorite part was that I had just done it—and so spontaneously! I really didn't care if I had missed the second leg of my flight or not. Whatever! It was almost August. I was back in the US. Believe it or not, my thoughts were like this: *I'll walk back to Boston if I have to, but I am in the mood to check out a ball game.* So I did, and so it goes! It's fascinating how life perspectives can change after challenging times. (Actually, I think this idea had initially been planted in my thoughts when Ferris, Cameron, and Sloane had taken in a Cubbies game nearly twenty years prior when they had stopped to take a look around.)

HELMETLESS HOME RUN

I used to lead the league in home runs in my backyard Wiffle ball field. I was also the only kid who played in every game and sometimes had twice as many "games played" as even the number two slugger. But I never actually hit a long ball in any real baseball game I had played in as a kid.

A believer in perseverance and longevity, I finally broke out of that homerless streak, but the one and only time I cleared the wall was a bit unique (of course). In 1997, at age twenty-five, I got selected to join the US Army baseball team in Korea. I was not yet in the Army but was one of the two civilians they would allow on the team (the other was a Canadian kid from Vancouver—he and I had been in Taegu, teaching English). We were the only non-Korean team in a twenty-team league, and it was especially honorable to wear our caps with "USA" stitched onto them.

On Opening Day during my first at bat—I suppose I felt the need to prove my worth and thus, keenly focused—I lofted a fly ball to left field. With a one-eared batting helmet (with cool-looking Korean advertising on the sides) on and thinking the ball was not hit so far, I chugged to first base with the thoughts of getting to second. My helmet flew off at about the same time it was evident that the ball had cleared the Marine Corps barracks in left field. Home run! Legitimate home run! I got to do a trot. Me! Finally! A glorious home run trot! I had only seen those being done by others. Here I am, a quarter-century old, and I finally get to do my own—but with no helmet on. Oh well, put it in the books. I wouldn't trade the memory for anything!

RAT! RAT! IN LYNN

Fraser Field in Lynn was undergoing renovations to spiff up the old baseball stadium for the Mass Mad Dogs. This independent minor league team was due to begin to play there the following season. The construction was significant but usable in the meantime. So we used it. I pitched for a twilight men's league team called the Kingston Night Owls, based out of Kingston, New Hampshire, which was not too far from Lynn but quite a different town than what Lynn had become by the late '90s. Though I never lived in New Hampshire, I would drive to the games and meet the team wherever the schedule took us.

One night, we were using the dugout along the first base line. Interestingly, that dugout was immediately below the old grandstands, but because of work being done to expand the area, the back wall of the dugout was removed entirely. Then, what that looked like was us sitting there on the same old bench, but behind us was the under dwellings of this then-fifty-six-year-old structure with remnants and fossils of old wrappers and cups and scorecards and sunflower seeds and popcorn kernels and matches from spectators' cigars. Because it was a night game, there was no light shining in there at all. Had I seen a horror movie in the day or two prior, I might not have rested so easily while sitting there.

In the middle innings, a line drive foul ball blazes past us, into that darkness. Anyone who has ever played or been to a men's league ball game knows that all balls are retrieved. We treat them like they're our car keys. We pay for those, so unless the stitches are coming out, we find it and put it back in play. We also have an unwritten roster of who goes and gets the ball. This time, it was my turn. Luckily, I had watched the ball land, though it was a good fifty feet behind us, into the darkness. I was not a massive fan of spiders and that kind of thing, but it helped that I couldn't see webs or any of that matter well enough.

I went back, got the ball and then developed a really bright idea as I turned and made my way back. A couple of unassuming teammates were talking, looking out at the field of play, backs turned to me. These guys were good-natured and could be as much of the joker I liked to be. *Here we go,* I thought. "I am going to scare the absolute bejesus out of these two." I started screaming "rat!" and running toward the light, the dugout, safety—where they were. I thought this was a hoot; these two are going to get up and bust onto the playing field as if their lives depended on it. What kind of a hilarious scene am I about to inflame? We'll be talking about this one for years at holiday get-togethers! This may seem strange or even cruel, but this was baseball, and we did this shit all the time. It's one of the reasons we kept playing as adults. Where else can you go be competitive and die laughing, turning a blind eye to the struggles of the rest of your days, even if only for a few hours at a time?

Well, these guys never heard me as I kept yelling and running, amping up my game to follow through on my prank. When they finally turned to see what I was up to, I was lying on my back in the catcher's equipment bag. The joke was on me, ultimately. I failed to see the silhouette of the concrete overhang that made up the roof of the dugout structure. I nailed that thing so hard with my forehead that I honestly don't know how long I was out for in that adjacent bag of catching gear—and I had been running. My first memory was one of them casually saying, "Whitey, what the hell are you doing?" So we can retell the story, but it didn't turn out how I had initially thought it might! And that is why we love baseball. It offers so much, but it has no problem teaching you lessons and putting you precisely in your place!

STRIKE THREE?

I was the home plate umpire for a city high school baseball game at Clifford Playground in Roxbury on a spring afternoon in 2001. It was Fenway High versus J. D. O'Bryant. The pitcher and catcher tandem for Fenway was "swiss cheese" that day. I had to have gotten directly nailed by eight or nine wild pitches—I took shots in the shoulder, thigh, face mask, ankle. Finally, with two out and a full count on the O'Bryant batter, another errant pitch was ticketed to become my tenth bruise and was heading dead center for my nose. I just couldn't stand there one more time. I flinched. More accurately, I completely closed my eyes and jerked my head off to the right.

Oh, (expletive)! I thought. *I have no idea what the batter did.* It was ball four, no doubt, but did he swing? Beats me! Earlier that year, I had gone to Florida and attended the Jim Evans Academy of Professional Umpiring. I was aware of a few ball/strike-call protocols. For example, a called ball should only be audible to the batter and catcher, a called strike shall be heard by both benches, and a swinging strike is a silent fist pump. I had nothing on this one though. Thankfully, the catcher did catch the ball, so I was spared, and my call options were limited. I took a moment and observed how the players reacted. The batter turned and walked away, so he must have swung. On cue, I gave a nonchalant raised fist clench as if I had seen it all along. I guess it was strike three! "Let's go now. Hustle out!" I barked out (and rolled my eyes for only me to see).

INSTANT KARMA AND CANDY

If you know me, you know I love baseball (understatement?). Of course, I love all the parts of the great pastime: the smell of the dirt and the cut grass, the sound of the wood bat connecting with a well-pitched ball, the stitches against my fingers when I am about to bend off a slider, seeing a teammate hustle down a tough liner toward the gap. You name it! I love the game. But when things get into full-on competition mode, the sweetest of all things is karma, especially instant karma, in your favor.

Here is my favorite personal experience with that:

Seabrook, New Hampshire, 1996

I played for the Kingston Night Owls in a men's league comprised of teams on the Massachusetts-New Hampshire border area. I was pitching. There were two outs, and I gave up a solidly hit line-drive single to left field. As the batter made his way to first, he said loudly enough for me to hear, "That's like taking candy from a baby!" Naturally, whatever form of pissed I felt for having given up the hit immediately elevated to anger when I recognized that he was remarking about my offering. I took it personally.

When I got the ball back, I returned to the rubber. I looked over to the now-runner on first, and to my amazement, he was five feet off the bag, leading toward second base, and looking down at his waist, tucking his batting gloves into his belt. *For real? What a prima donna?* I thought. I chucked the ball to my first baseman and nailed the guy—inning over!

Still on the mound, I yelled at him at the top of my lungs: "There's your f—— candy, pal!" I don't know whose little nieces were there that night, but I hope they read this now and figure out what that was all about. I think that was the loudest I have ever yelled!

SECTION 3

CHILDHOOD

I divide my childhood into two parts: before and after we moved from Brockton to Maine. I was only seven when we moved, but I was an observant kid and I think I was more of a natural leader than I may have ever intended. We lived in three houses in Brockton in that short time. My parents had met there when my father moved in from Boston in his last year of high school as they were new neighbors. I was the oldest grandchild on both sides of the family. I had four grandparents with five uncles and three aunts who were all under the age of twenty-three and were present when I came to being fifty years ago at the Brockton Hospital. I had a sister who was less than two years younger than me. My father was a self-employed carpenter, and my mother stayed home with us, saved for some part-time work she did with the Brockton Credit Union and then a local real estate agency. We had a three-legged black dog who had been hit by a car after she leaped out of the back of my father's pickup truck bed and had blindly bolted across the thoroughfare that is Brockton's Montello Street and two cats. We were close. I thrived, and I loved it.

Most of my free time in Brockton was spent doing just about anything with my neighborhood friends. We were often gathering up leftover scraps of wood to use to build a makeshift fort. We used rocks as hammers and tried to put the frame together with a pile of roofing nails I would get from my dad. We played cops and robbers and cowboys and Indians. We would go to Fischer's Market and get rolls and rolls of red caps for our cap guns. We would creatively find ways to detonate each lovely little gunpowder-filled circle. We ate ten-cent sticks of sour apple Jolly Rancher. We collected Charlie's Angels cards, climbed trees, buzzed around the side streets on Big Wheels, communicated with walkie-talkies, called the safe zone in tag "ghouls," and plotted out strategies to protect the neighborhood from rival enemy neighborhoods. We watched the *Three Stooges* on Channel 38 and would play out their antics in our real lives. We never had money to chase down the ice cream truck but would get to get a sugar cone at the walk-up window at the next-door Friendly's when our grandmother came to visit. We always had put up a real Christmas tree and decorated it with medium-sized screw in colored lights and two or three boxes of silver tinsel. My sister and I shared a wood, hand-me-down bunk bed. We daydreamed through the annual Child World catalog about toy options to request from Santa when we visited him at the Westgate Mall. We attended Catholic mass weekly and celebrated every holiday with our extended family. We trick-or-treated, made big deals out of our birthdays (I always got Carvel ice cream cake), picnicked at D.W. Field Park, survived the Blizzard of '78, and watched the original Star Wars at the drive-in theater in Avon.

We moved to southern Seacoast Maine, two hours north of Brockton or about 76.9 miles from Gate A at Fenway Park in 1978. It was a challenging transition for me. For years after we went there, I would circle ads in the Boston Sunday Globe of houses for sale back in Massachusetts and put together pretty decent proposals to convince my parents we needed to return. The move also brought about a significant personal change: I had always been called Jay—since birth. But the day I rolled into the little old red schoolhouse in Ogunquit, midyear, the teacher introduced me to my second grade classmates as John. After all, I am John. But calling me "John" then was like completely changing my name. I might as well have become Mark or Dennis. John? Who the hell is John? Me! That's who I am! I was suddenly John, and I was not about to raise my hand and correct the almighty new teacher. I hated the limelight, and my one chance to change the trajectory of the name I would now go by had only a twenty-second window of time. I didn't stand up for myself. I let it go. I even bought into John. I understood. No one meant any harm. No one outside of family now even knew I was really Jay. So Maine John replaced Brockton Jay. Life could be way worse, which somehow, I feel like I already understood that then and consciously just chose to live with it.

I didn't know this at the time, but it turns out my friends and I were born smack dab in the middle of generation X. We used typewriters to do reports. If we had a working color TV, it was just ABC, NBC, CBS, and PBS for Sesame Street and the Electric Company. We watched cable TV move in, and we were attracted to MTV and ESPN. We collected returnable soda cans and exchanged every half dozen for a wax pack of Topps baseball cards. We joined Little League and did Cub Scouts. We played Wiffle ball all summer, tackle football with no pads in the fall, and pond hockey in the winter. Everyone had a bike and a landline phone. We chose a time and place to meet up and told our parents roughly when to expect to see us again. We ate peanut butter and jelly sandwiches or fluffernutters. We never carried water and rarely had a dime between us all. Almost every day included some sort of unplanned activity that turned out to be a great time.

What a great time in my life! As I get older, I recognize how great it was to be a child when I was with the friends I had in the place where we lived and given the opportunities that I was given. Life was good. It was safe, and we got what we needed. We were creative and learned how to navigate our world healthily.

THE DAY BUCKY DENT HOMERED

I was born and lived in Brockton, Massachusetts, until just after the start of second grade. After my father's family moved from Boston into a new development around the corner from my mother's home, my parents had met there on Cary Hill. I was the oldest grandchild on both sides, and my younger sister and I had our grandparents and three aunts and four uncles all living nearby. We were tight-knit, and it was quite an excellent way to start life.

My father was a self-employed carpenter who seemed to appreciate the quiet of working alone, having just returned from Vietnam two years before me being born. My mother stayed home with us. We had a dog and two cats, and we lived in a few different locations in Brockton—always in a triple-decker. My parents owned the last two multifamilies where we stayed and collected rent from the tenants who joined us. We went to St. Edwards Catholic School to start our education. Many of our days included playing in the yard with friends from the neighborhood, going to parks, swimming at the Montello Pool or at one of the South Shore's beaches, catching a little *Captain Kangaroo*, and enjoying our share of Apple Jacks and Spaghettios. Then one Sunday in the spring of 1978, just a few months removed from the great blizzard that sidelined us all for a few weeks, my father opened up the *Boston Globe* newspaper, and we discovered the inserted Red Sox color team photo. He told me about the new acquisitions: Dennis Eckersley from Cleveland and Mike Torrez from the Yankees. It seems like that same day, though I know enough about memory mashing time together, and this certainly could have been weeks or a month after getting the team picture, my father showed me how to read the standings. In our hometown paper, the Red Sox were always listed in capital letters (BOSTON). The other six teams in the American League East were written "normally": Toronto, Milwaukee, New York, Cleveland, Baltimore, Detroit. The moment I understood how these standings worked was the moment I got absolutely hooked on baseball. My father had no idea what kind of monster he was letting out of the closet. I became a die-hard fan immediately.

Of course, having the team Boston had then made it pretty easy to get wrapped up in them: Hall of Famers Carl Yastrzemski, Jim Rice, and Carlton Fisk, plus guys who were perennial all-stars: Fred Lynn, Rick Burleson, Dwight Evans, George Scott, Bill Lee, and Luis Tiant. (Eck made the Hall too, but I attribute that to what he did later with the Oakland A's). I can rattle off all of these guys' names still, faster than I can name any other Boston edition and probably quicker than I could name the kids in my class then, or even the names of my aunts and uncles. I knew all of their numbers (and still do—ask). I could mimic their batting stances or unique throwing motions. I even used to grab a wad of Sun-Maid raisins to make it look like chewing tobacco lodged in the side of my cheek (thank you, Pudge). I got the hat. I got the replica helmet. I even asked for and received a pair of red spikes for my seventh birthday that year—because the Red Sox wore red spikes. My father and I watched games on TV and listened to the non-televised ones on the radio. I got my friends into the Sox. We all got hooked on the weekly national program *This Week in Baseball.* I was introduced to the what-seemed-foreign National League (I recall those pillbox caps worn by Dave Parker and that rainbow jersey of the Houston Astros. *Who were those strange teams?* I remember thinking).

That summer turned out to be a barn burner locally. Quite honestly, I have learned more about it in the years since than I even realized at the time. In 1978, I was starstruck. But I knew the Yankees were the enemy, and I knew the two teams had a hell of a battle all summer, though that part of the rivalry hadn't bitten my soul yet. (This was probably the last summer I was mature about the Yankees and Red Sox.) I know the Sox blew a monumental lead in the standings, then blew a big series at Fenway later in the summer. I also know Boston needed to—and did—win their final eight games of the regular season to have a shot at catching the Yankees—and that happened. Back then, only the winner of the division moved on to the playoffs. There was no such thing as a wild card. The American League (AL) and National League (NL) each had two divisions—the East and the West. The Kansas City Royals had won the West in the AL. After the 162-game schedule had concluded, the New York Yankees and the Boston Red Sox were dead even: ninety-nine wins to sixty-three losses. A coin toss had decided game 163 would be played in our state, at Fenway Park, on October 2.

Here is where the story gets wonky. October 2 was not just arguably the biggest game of the decade for all of baseball, but it might have also been the biggest game in Red Sox history and in the history of Fenway Park. October 2 was also the day we moved from Brockton to a rural seaside town in southern Maine, one hundred miles away and eighty miles the other side of the Green Monster. Our TV had been unplugged, packed, and sent away already. My father had taken off early and headed to the new house. My mother and aunt waited behind, and my sister and I were with them. Because of the move, we did not have to go to school. Many of the neighbors seemed to be home and skipping work that day and had the afternoon game on TV. We walked down the street and quickly got updates. The last thing I remember is that the Red Sox were up 1–0 on a Yaz home run. The people on the right, halfway down Laurel Ave. yelled that out to us. Things seemed promising for the Old Towne Team. After receiving that positive report, our time to vacate the apartment came, and we climbed in our Olds metallic baby-blue Delta 88 and headed to Maine midgame. We drove through Boston, not far from Fenway. We left behind our wider family. We left behind my school. We left behind my classmates and my friends. We left behind Bucky Dent. We left behind a tragic ending. For years, I had hated Torrez for giving up that home run to that Yankees' shortstop. And I hated the diminutive shortstop for hitting that home run. It wasn't until a few years later that I realized this hate was wrong and irrational. This was not Mike Torrez's fault, and this was not something incredible by B. F. Dent! This was my fault as I should never have left the great Commonwealth. I have carried this burden for far too long! Now maybe you can better understand why, when you see me yelling at my kids, "Wait a minute, the game is almost over… Hold on!" after they have been pleading with me, "Dad, you have nothing to do with the outcome of the Red Sox's (or Patriots') games," I am the way I am.

(After years of reflection, penance paid by working for four years at Fenway and rolling up that nasty-smelling Turface-filled multiton tarp on cold rainy nights, moving back to and residing in the Bay State again, having to deal with two more great Sox tragedies in 1986 and 2003, and finally, the curse was broken. None was happier or more relieved than I. I think I am actually pretty synonymous with the Red Sox in the eyes of just about anyone who knows me. I think if asked to tell something they know about me, family and friends would quickly suggest that I am the biggest Red Sox fan they have ever met. But I had to be. It was not a choice but a calling.

PINEWOOD NICKELS

To immerse me in kid-dom upon moving to Maine in second grade, aside from school, I played Little League baseball, went to Sunday School at St. Mary's, and joined the Cub Scouts. The Cub Scouts was a good time. My mother even became the assistant den pack, big cub leader. We did all sorts of activities—we toured an ambulance, made giant Easter egg decorations, painted the Wells Harbor dock, sold Tom Watt products, and enjoyed making costumes for the Halloween party. My father pitched in too—like the time he and I made a teeth-staining blue-dyed cake for the annual Blue and Gold banquet. But most memorable (and character-building of all) was the Pinewood Derby.

Anyone who has participated in a Pinewood Derby may know that there are certain weight and size standards that your car is to be made into—from the original block of wood that you are issued. The Pinewood Derby becomes as much a fashion show as it is a race. The Derby is designed for scouts to spend time with a parent or adult who can create a fantastic finished product. Well, Dad has worked with wood all of his adult life—whether as a carpenter or a high school shop teacher. Dad is naturally quite crafty. However, though I didn't incorporate this, I think it now: he was only a decade removed from some tumultuous time in Vietnam, and he had always maintained an edgy attitude.

Moving midyear in second grade unlocked a shyness in me that lasted for years. At the date of that first Pinewood Derby, the shy Jay White was in full bloom, and my shyness was highly evidenced by my redder-than-red face and ears. Coupled with what I just mentioned, there was a silent sideshow creeping in from under the radar—unbeknownst to all. (Who are these new people?) Instead of carving out a curved hood, we used wood-bonding material (illegal!). Instead of using the included lead pellets, which were to be melted down and then embedded into the vehicle to get the car up to specs, my father bore a hole (in the hood/Bondo), and he brought a pocketful of nickels with us to the post office before the event. The postal clerk agreed to weigh our car, and it called for five nickels (illegal!) to make weight. Dad glued the nickels together and then into the borehole. What a unique look! Off to the Ward Gym, we went to join my new friends in the community gymnasium for the event of the year in Cub Scout land.

I think the scoutmaster, or whoever the leaders were, recognized my quiet shyness and kindly allowed me to race my unsanctioned but creatively customized development that day. They probably made an agreement that I could not win the golden trophy, but what damage would there be to let the new kid participate with all the other kids? Well, lo and behold, our car was allowed to race! *Dad knows what he is doing,* I probably thought. We kept winning. Kids were fascinated by this one-of-a-kind dark horse, and I was starting to like the positive attention. Then though, the adhesive began to weaken. One race, at least halfway through the event, one nickel flew off when the car stopped.

"Oh shit!" I didn't say then but would have if my forty-nine-and-a-half-year-old self could have filled in the verbal gaps for that eight-year-old boy then. In the next heat, all five nickels came loose, and, of course, they rolled akimbo. I can still hear the sound of those five-cent pieces scattering on that lonely hardwood floor, moving for what seemed like forever in all directions. Everyone laughed. My car had become the favorite item of the day. Those kids helped me retrieve the coins. I became filled with embarrassment. Let the redness begin! I could feel the blood rushing to my cheeks, forehead, neck, and ears. Now this really allowed kids to notice me. It seemed my car was then in every other round from then on. I could no longer care less about the Pinewood Derby as I just wanted to be out of there. But, like torture, mounting that car on top of the sloop and placing that stack of then-loose nickels in that hole only to watch them inevitably spread broader and broader in their roll across the floor when the car reached the end of the track, I was gaining all sorts of character.

So I guess that event did have quality and value. Now I tend to be compassionate to others, and I would never publicly embarrass anyone. I am also slow to bend the rules and never like to grab too much attention. I think all of those things have helped me in this thing called life. Thanks, Dad! (He probably knew what he was doing. That's how he is!)

OGUNQUIT FISHING DERBY

In the spring of 1979, I stood on the grassy embankment of Moody Pond, which is alongside Route One in Ogunquit, Maine. I was almost eight years old, and I was attending the annual fishing derby there. My family had moved to this area the previous fall, and I was kind of a shy kid—or I certainly did not appreciate any limelight or too much attention in public. I also didn't know how to fish.

It was a Saturday, and my Dad, a self-employed carpenter, was at work. My mother had driven me to the pond in our Olds Delta 88 (we would joke that that car put the "old" in Oldsmobile). But she needed to take my little sister and even younger cousin back home to use the bathroom (Edison didn't invent the Porta-Potty for another decade, I think.) Of course, they were gone for way too long. I figured the car must have broken down—it did. (What was the plan? No phones. No way to let my parents know I might be stranded. Imagine? This was the norm. Nothing was too unusual—even leaving an eight-year-old alone to fish.)

Back to where the story gets its memory. Not really wanting to jab the nasty hook through the worm I had, I loosely pretzel-tied the worm around the hook. Somehow it seemed to work. At this age, I really didn't care about catching a fish so much as I cared about not looking clueless to my new second-grade classmates who were all there too. Finally, I went to cast that setup into the water. I had my thumb on the release. I looked behind me to make sure no one was in my range. All clear! Pole in the air and fling. The line did not extend, but it did swing around. A shocking and stabbing pain immediately entered my right nostril. The worm stayed on! But the worm, which I could blurrily see in my lower peripheral, was dangling from my nose. The hook was embedded in me. Damn, did that hurt! Putting the pole down only pulled at the catch—me. So I realized that one of my hands was rendered useless insofar as a player in the release effort as I had to keep slack on the line. Pulling out something from oneself, especially under the age of ten, is not usually so easy. But when the battle of physical pain meets up with the struggle of emotional distress, I had no problem yanking that hook out of my inner nose. To this day, I remain the biggest thing I have ever caught!

POTTY AND PRICE

Growing up Catholic in New England, when my sister and I were little and would have Necco Wafers, we would save the white ones. We then played "church" and pretended we were the priest. We'd hold it up high with both hands. Never really knowing what the priest had been saying to all of those adults when we would accompany our parents to the altar on Sundays, we would say "potty and price" as we handed the candy to the other.

THE FRED LYNN BALL

It was 1980, and my dad and I had gone to see the Sox play at Fenway Park one summer Sunday afternoon. After the game, we stood on Van Ness Street, outside the gate to the player's parking lot, waiting to catch a glimpse of the greats: Jim Rice, Carlton Fisk, Butch Hobson, Eck, Yaz, Dewey Evans, or anyone from the team. Police yelled and whistled to alert fans to make way as they pushed aside the wooden Boston police barricade so various players could exit in their vehicles (I seem to recall that Hobson drove a yellow pickup truck). Noticing my good behavior, he had told me, one cop rewarded me with a baseball. He said that that had been a ball that Fred Lynn had fouled off during the day's game. I was thrilled! Dad and I drove back to our home in Wells, Maine. Later that week, using the slightly cracked Carl Yastrzemski-model bat that Jim Rice had given me when we had visited spring training in Winter Haven, Dad parked that Fred Lynn ball into the woods behind our yard when we played one-on-one baseball. We never found the ball. As I recall, I was not that upset as I was at least as much impressed by my dad's prowess at the plate. (Though we may never find the ball, capturing the memory in writing brings on a whole new value.)

(DON'T) TAKE ME OUT TO THE BALL GAME

My father has the habit of saying "can't" instead of "can" in certain situations. For example, he might say, "Hey, why don't we head down to Fenway to see if we can't get some Red Sox tickets." Well, one time it was still winter, and being the die-hard Sox fan who is never going to say no to such an offer (even if grammatically, saying "no" would be a double-negative—forget it, whatever), I agreed. We should definitely do that. I think it must have been a Saturday, and we were both wanting to wish the remainder of winter away and welcome back the Boys of Summer. We lived in Wells, Maine, and Fenway is about seventy miles away. So we hopped in his truck and headed to Boston. When we got there, the ticket office was all closed up. It was not open for another week. We were okay with this though, for some reason. In fact, we still crack up and recount the time we went to see if "we can't get tickets," and we successfully couldn't get tickets. Nothing like doing all you set out to do!

LADIES AND GENTLEMEN, A RARE POEM ABOUT COTTAGE CHEESE

Cheese is great. I love cheese.
Hot pizza cheese: the more, the merrier.
When the mood is right, Friday night,
Can't get enough.
But I don't like cottage cheese.
Uncle Bill killed a cottonmouth, in Arkansas, with a spade.
Its head came off, and the neck spewed what looked like cottage cheese.
I don't care if I never eat cottage cheese again. That was 1976.

BOOK FORTHCOMING

I was a terrible student in junior high school and high school. In eighth grade, I did miserably on oral book reports…until I decided to go rogue. I totally faked the name of an author and book title and told a real-life story to my class. It was my first and only *A*. (I was really nervous the teacher would ask me to see the book.)

WHEN I WAS MO CHEEKS

"What did you use to do when you were a kid?" You want to know one thing I did on any random weeknight in the winter? Well, among other things, sometimes I was the Nuggets versus the Jazz. Followed by the Suns versus Sonics. On good nights, I got to be Celtics-Sixers or Pistons-Lakers. So WAY BACK, even before dial-up (sorry for the sound I just provided to probably at least half of you), it was me plus time plus imagination plus a Nerf hoop.

I took out a notebook and listed every NBA team (yes, Sonics was a team; they are now the Oklahoma City Thunder. The Grizzlies, Heat, Raptors, Timberwolves, Magic, Hornets, and now-Pelicans did not exist. The Clippers might have been San Diego still, and the Wizards were definitely the Bullets—can I still say that? The Nets were in Jersey. I digress). Then I matched them each up and set my clock radio alarm for four four-minute quarters. I stood back about ten feet, made a "jump shot" worth two points, and followed the shot. Anything rebounded or caught exiting the net but before reaching the ground was fair game for an additional one. So it would be me, as Philly's Mo Cheeks shooting from downrange. I would suddenly morph into Dr. J to get the rebound and dunk it for the additional point. Three-nothing, 76ers. The Celtics would immediately be up next. Me/Bird for two! Chief with the catch-and-dunk! We're all tied up, with three minutes and forty-nine to go in the first quarter. This went on for hours many nights every week.

I am curious: Did my parents wonder what all that noise was, especially that goddamn alarm going off eight to ten times during one episode of M*A*S*H*? Oh well, I gained a valuable life skill: I am an excellent Nerf basketball rebounder! I promise to mention that in my next interview.

MASS BEFORE MASS

I was a self-proclaimed pretty easy kid to please growing up. The absolute sweetest thing I could have possibly heard back in the early to mid-1980s was when my father would ask if I felt like going to the next day's Red Sox game. Are you kidding me? I pretty much lived for the Red Sox, even when it was not so popular to do. Well before "Sweet Caroline" and Big Papi and all the duck boat celebrations, we had a wicked Curse, organ music, and Stan Papi. At that time, you could roll up to any of the ticket booths inside Gate A on Yawkey Way, put down a ten, and get two grandstand seats. We always seemed to get a pair for Section 1 or 2—deep right field—and then had a mastery of scoring box seats near the on-deck circle (that's a story for another day).

But then there was sometimes the "Sunday Conflict!" First of all, we were now residents of Wells, Maine, by the time my deep love for the Sox had come about. Wells to Fenway is about seventy miles or so. Though it is a relatively straight shot down I-95 with a connection onto Route 1, there would typically be traffic on the Mystic River Bridge or Storrow Drive and most definitely at Kenmore Square (for those of you from out of town, Kenmore is where the Citgo sign is mounted). A day at the ballpark for us included being there when the gates opened, watch as much batting practice as possible, take in the game and then wait outside the team parking lot for a chance to see the players up close afterward. So we really needed to be "on the hop." All was good unless it was the day the Lord made. "Johnny, you two should really go to Mass (we're talking church as in Catholic Mass—not Massachusetts—here) first!" my mother would painfully but logically interject, telling my father what her wishes for me were to be.

Noooo! I would think. *Church? No way!*

"He is about to make his confirmation. You can go to 'The Nine' before you go to see the Red Sox!" she would say. Oh my goodness. What would happen if we didn't go? What if we said yes to her but then just drove straight to the ball game instead (and just never told her)? Would the Sox lose because of us? What would happen? Would I have been restricted to choosing lesser-than saint names for my confirmation? After all, let's face it: confirmation is a time to add a spicy new name to your moniker and then what else? Proving I will go to church for the next umpteen Sundays? Well, not wanting to be stuck as John William "Bartholomew" White Jr., we ducked into St. Mary's and prayed for haste those Sundays. Never did the Apostles' Creed seem so slow and long as it did when I could smell peanuts and popcorn and hear John Kiley's National Anthem being cued up.

"I believe in one holy Catholic and apostolic church," everyone would slowly recite. I was like: "I believe Tony Perez might get the nod over Yaz at first base today. Let's get outta here!" Did we shake hands with everyone yet? Was that last week? Come on, come on, come on. "Yeah, yeah, peace be with you! And also with you, and you over there!" I would say and/or think. "Dad, when we go up for the host, let's just walk to the car from there. Cool?" And that's what we did. A little compromise never killed anyone. Plus, our answer to the big question: Did you at least stay for the Eucharist? was a tried-and-true yes! That question was like "1b" when we arrived home at the end of the day—right after "Did they win?"

SECTION 4

HIGH SCHOOL

By the time high school rolled around for me, I had realized I was no academic. I didn't like to read. I didn't do well in math. I only got grades good enough so I could play baseball in the spring. In the spring, I would then fail the semester and at my parochial school and become ineligible for fall sports. I showered and dressed neatly because I usually had some girl I had been interested in, even though I was too insecure to ever let her know so much. I had to go to summer school for English class my junior year. I worked in the summers but had little money remaining by winter and would drive my hand-me-down Toyota Celica on fumes. Before long, I learned that my favorite activity in school was entertaining others. I realized that I loved to make people laugh, and I did so at the expense of good grades. But after all, I accomplished my goal in high school: not to drop out. Dropping out would have caused too many problems, and I was too fragile to handle the names tagged onto high school dropouts.

SUCKER PUNCHED

I was reaching into my locker.
Somewhere in there was my earth science t…
Yellow light. Outlined in red.
A sharp pain tunneled through my brain—from one ear to the other.
A boy and a girl and maybe another couple of people yelped.
I did not know why they did that.
I quickly faced to my left without me turning my head.
Some senior, the kid with BMX bunny-hop forearms, had nailed me in the right jaw.
We had never spoken before. Or since.
I knew who he was, but only by default.
There was no ill will that I can imagine.
He just decided to blow his steam on an unsuspecting freshman.
I could not eat for a week.
Who knew the pain that came with salivary gland release into a damaged TMJ?
The smell of food released a sharp internal liquidy pain.
I did not cry at school. The day that happened, I wanted to.
The principal approached me three days later. I declined to take action (of course, this was the '80s).
I never told my parents (don't worry. If you read this today, I am okay with the whole thing).
But that day, I made up my mind.
The following year, I agreed to go to the Catholic school my mom had wanted me to go to.

THE FOREIGN EXCHANGE STUDENT

When my sister was in eighth grade, she took part in a foreign exchange program with her French language class, and we had this girl, Francine, from Quebec stay at our house for a week. My sister, or none of us for that matter, could not speak a lick of French, and Frannie didn't speak a lick of English. (We were done after bonjour, *je m'appelle*, and Les Canadiens, Les Nordiques, and au bon pain.) But that did not stop my sister from trying.

By the end of the week, the girls had something in common with their language. *How wonderful!* you might think. No. By Friday, we couldn't understand either one of them. When my sister asked Frannie questions, she remained in full-on English but just decided to add an arbitrary French accent to the words: "Ehhh, Ah-nie? You like a pizza? Z-pizza?" And that's how that went.

NATIVE AMERICAN SATS

In high school in the late '80s, you had to take the Scholastic Aptitude Test (SAT) if you wanted to have any shot of getting admitted to a college. When you had subpar grades as I had had, the SAT was kind of an opportunity to collect a golden nugget—a Hail Mary touchdown, if you will—to show prospective schools you might have more to offer than your 2.0 GPA (1.7 rounded up). Some kids who were hell-bent on going to college were known to take that damn test multiple times to best their score. Not me. I was a one-and-done kind of kid, and I thought, *What you get is what you get. Take me if you want me* (same kinda attitude I still carry today). But I got butterflies on the day of the exam.

I arrived at my high school basketball gymnasium on time. I had my two No. 2 Dixon-Ticonderoga pencils all sharpened up and ready to go. I sat in my assigned seat and waited until the proctors reported that the test may begin. It was common knowledge (or was it an urban legend?) that you would at least get a few hundred points just by correctly completing the demographics section. *That's cool. Some no-brainer points, which is like scoring an uncontested layup*, I thought. Whoa! Easy, pal! I got to race, looked at my options, and began to sweat that cold sweat that only a high school kid can sweat—more fearful of making a fool of himself than worrying about what college he goes to someday. I didn't know which corresponding circle to fill in. I knew I wasn't Black. I knew I wasn't Asian. I indeed was not Pacific Islander or Alaskan. My choices were dwindling. My sweat was building. Others' pencils were down. I had a blank section. My layup was about to rattle off the rim. If I didn't fill out something, I was destined to flip burgers forever without this gimme two hundred supposed points. Anyone who looked up saw I was not done yet! I had to get this hot potato pencil out of my hand. AHHH!

I remember teachers had suggested taking your time and eliminating the answers you knew are wrong. I had already done that. Two choices remained. Caucasian was one of my options. I saw Asian at the end of the word, but I had never seen that word before. I tried to sound it out: cah-OOK-ASIAN. Immediately, I realized, *No way! I don't know what a Caucasian is, but I know I'm not one of them.* Finally, I settled on Native American. In fact, I justified my thoughts. *I was born in Brockton, Massachusetts, America! I'm a native of Brockton! Hello!* It came upon me like midnight clear. Of course, Native American. How did it take me so long to make that choice? Wow! Well, it's been a long time coming, but once I learned what a Caucasian was, I have wanted to apologize to my Native friends for the dip in their average scores in 1988!

UH-OH, SPAGHETTIOS!

It's almost Rockwellian and certainly a "slice of Americana" to think of having lunch at another kid's house. I envision images (or advertisements, I suppose) of Annette Funicello pitching Skippy peanut butter or choosy moms choosing Jif, or the kid spelling out what brand of bologna he puts on his sandwich and how good Fritos go with lunch. There is a time when having lunch at home, or especially at "another kid's home," abruptly ends, and ye hardly even know that day would be all she wrote.

The last time I did (I will say "almost did") have lunch at another kid's house was memorable. But since it has been proven that I am no longer a kid and that was indeed the last time a friend's parent agreed to make lunch for us, I know there are four of us who stand outside the norm by recalling their last time.

My friend Chris, who was the star and teammate of my high school baseball team, and his sister Val, who I took to the prom earlier that year, had my sister, Alisa, who was two grades behind me, and I over to their house one early summer day. I cannot recall why we all had quite so much free time on the same day, but we tried to be together as often as possible when we did. Around noon, their dad came home early from his job in neighboring Portsmouth one of those days. Ever-friendly and supportive of his two kids, Mr. Plante agreed to make us lunch. "You guys want some Spaghettios?" he asked. Now I know Chris and I were pushing eighteen or at least high school graduation, and there was a general feeling that at that time and by that age, we should want to appear more mature than Spaghettio-eating giant children. But we were just kids still, and who doesn't want a parent (or the other kids' parent) to make them a hot bowl of Spaghettios? (In fact, I would still enjoy it, and fifty is now so close I can track its delivery on Amazon.) I believe the collective answer from the four of us was an emphatic "yeah!"

Mr. Plante, always known for giving me gruff for my love of the Red Sox and his muttering that "they'll never win, John, never!" (I thought of him right away back in 2004 and '07 and 2013 and 2018, but I digress), liked to store extra cans of nonperishables in the basement. So almost proud of himself that he could so easily just go downstairs and appear with a can or two of that delicious then-Franco-American treat, Mr. Plante took out a pot, put it on the stove, and grabbed the handheld can opener. He seemed genuinely happy to have us all there, almost as if he recognized that the days of making his own kids and their friends lunch was reaching the finish line.

When Mr. Plante depressed the opener into the lid of that can, it sounded like the house had been struck by a drive-by shooter. "Boom!" It appeared that the can's entire contents had found their way to the ceiling, save for the particular saucy-noodled debris that caught Mr. Plante first. One second, we were all relaxed and enjoying the thought of the forthcoming mouth-watering, time-tested, kid-approved bowl of love. Then, almost as if this was the moment itself that thrust the four of us into adulthood, Mr. Plante barked out, "Make your own goddamn lunch!" I don't recall what we ended up doing for lunch that day, but seeing a ripped C-shaped Spaghettio dangling from Mr. Plante's right eyebrow, held on by the gluey sauce, was about the last thing I remember. Because from that visual on, I went into my now-is-not-the-time-to-laugh mode, and the memory stopped there. But better than any bowl of old-school Spaghettios would have been, the thirty-plus-year-old memory holds much more worth. It still cracks me up!

R FOR RIDE

It was the beginning of the junior year in high school, and I was ready to get my driver's license. My parents sent us to a Catholic school in New Hampshire, twenty-one miles away from our home in Maine. You could make an argument that even though I was just a teenager, having a license was as necessary as any other commuter, adult or otherwise. Our family had a manual transmission Ford Escort, with which I used to train. I got pretty good with the clutch and changing gears, all that. I was eager to gain independence. It was really a drag to get a ride with a friend's mother. I was tired of having to wait for an hour after practice, watching hundreds of sets of headlights come down Dover Point Road to the point where I was so mesmerized a couple of UFOs could have snuck in there and zoomed by me until someone would be back to pick me up.

Finally, the date for my exam was set. As the law would have it, I had to go back to Maine to take the test there. Nothing was convenient in Maine then, so I had to go to the town of Sanford, not even the town we lived in, to test. My mother drove me and dropped me off. I had to use the state's vehicle though as my mother was using the Escort that day and could not free up our car. One might think I lucked out to get to test on an automatic, but this is not what I was used to at this point. An actual police officer did the testing. He was very robotic and quite stern. He did not care to talk with me or calm my nerves. He was a just-the-facts-ma'am type of guy. I got intimidated by him and then started realizing my freedom stood between me and the other side of him. "Directionals! Show me the right directional!" he belched out from in front of the hood, standing on the street. (My thoughts: *You mean* blinker*? That's right: directional = blinker*). Boom. I flipped the right directional on, then the left. D-U-

N, done! Now what? A couple more exterior items happened. (Lights maybe? High beams?)

Officer got in, buckled up. I was already buckled. I waited to adjust the mirrors so he could see me do it and not think I had forgotten. So I did that—rearview first, right side, left side. Pretty much ready to go. He has the dreadful clipboard on his lap and snaps a black ink pen into action. After a pause, he finally commanded, "When you think you're ready, go ahead and pull away." I quietly inhale a little and then exhale.

I thought, *Oh boy. Here we go. You got this*, I reminded myself. The first move: left foot swings and missed at the nonexistent clutch that they don't have in an automatic. Did he even see that though? I could pull that off as me getting prepared/comfortable/ready to be a mature driver on the mean streets of Sanford, Maine. Next, I finally got to make my first (next?) big move. I readied my right hand and reached down to the shifter. I saw *P*, *R*, *N*, something, something else, more. He got me. I was so intimidated that I could not think nimbly. *What does all of this mean?* P*?* R*?* N*?* R2D2*! Shit! I know what it means. It all looks so familiar. But I am used to* P, R, *1, 2, 3, 4* quickly but somehow slowly at the same time crossed through my mind. I knew the worst thing I could have done was do nothing though as any delay on my behalf would have thrown up a giant red flag. If there was one thing this tester dude did not care about, it was when John William White Jr., DOB: May 29, 1971 got his f——in license. So it's me versus the world. Here we go. Hope shines in. *Oh, I know. That's it,* I thought of it. It came to me: R. R *means* ride*! Of course it does.* So I threw that bad boy into ride. Whew! Now we're ready to get this ordeal started and one laminated license in the pocket of this new driver. Ride? There is no "ride." The car, who cared about me getting my license about as much as my police officer buddy did, followed my directions and did not hear me think ride as in "hey, let's go forward." Settled in *R*, I double-checked my left side and made sure it was super safe to pull out—foot to the accelerator. Depress the pedal. Then the sickest feeling I had had in my seventeen-year life happened next: the Impala rushed to the rear against my will, behind my back, and against anything I could have imagined.

Oh no! That's it! I failed. I failed immediately. I failed abruptly. Maine was strict with these things. Three more months of schlepping with other people's mothers for my two-hundred-plus-miles-a-week commute just to go to high school! I remember going to bed that night, thinking, *How do I tell my buddies about this? They all know I was testing on this day.* Well, thank God they all love to laugh! I can still hear the roar of Brian Fogarty and see the milk spitting out of Paul Fenton's mouth that following day in the cafeteria when I recited my exploits. Did we laugh! So to ease the pain even more, I hope you laughed at it again in 2021!

SECTION 5

COLLEGE

I graduated with a degree in communications. However, I had owed so much money. When I opened the graduation binder, I found a note demanding I contact the registrar before vacating the campus instead of a diploma. In fact, three years would pass before I had to plead with an administrative staff member to issue me a certification required as part of my being hired to teach English in South Korea with the agreement that I would begin to pay off a sizable chunk of my debt.

As I look back on college, it wasn't so much that I learned useful material via classroom instruction that I became better equipped to handle adversity and even failure. I tried out for the baseball team there all four years. Each time I tried out, I worked hard to improve myself from the previous year. So the disappointment was as intense every time. But I worked through that. I did a good job learning how to be more social with a diverse group of people. I battled homesickness with a positive attitude, and those life skills have been invaluable.

YOU KILLED ME, SHEEN

Sometimes the funniest memories come from the times that laughing felt inappropriate. Sometimes, those moments may not have even been the most humorous of times, but the fact that you could not or should not be laughing is what makes it so fantastic—but only years later. In fact, at the moment, the laughter itself is mixed with a heavy dose of fear (of whatever—retribution, punishment, embarrassment—you name it).

By no means is the scene where Charlie Sheen flips an olive out of his girlfriend's belly button in *Hot Shots!* on any of the lists of the silver screen's most comical moments. But while lying on the floor with my grandmother right behind me, thinking she may not appreciate this, I must have burned three thousand calories as my body silently shook and gyrated to the hilarity of our situation. I have a pretty good spider sense, and I would bank on the fact that I was not alone with the silent gyrating—the room was way too quiet for the scene. I mean, an appropriate response by ordinary viewers would have been a chuckle, at least. But our painful silence indicated the moment had taken on much more humor to everyone else as well. I would go to great lengths to not disappoint my grandmother. So the fact that Mimi, who had a wonderful sense of humor but who I imagined thought that movie scenes like this fell into a tomfoolery category, was watching this—or better yet, watching me watch this—made this painful. But I loved every second of it, especially now! I mean, the sound of that ice cube's melting water dropping in there. Stop! You're killing me, Sheen!

(I googled it today. The *Hot Shots!* scene is called "Food of Love." Check it out. Imagine my scene. Makes me remember the moment like it happened last week.)

THE CANOEING SPIDER

My sister was two grades behind me in school and still in New England when I had left to go to college in Central Florida. Having visited me on a few occasions, she decided to apply and enroll too. So when she got there, I was happy to introduce her to a few of the activities I had enjoyed and experienced. I imagine that when most people think of Florida, the travel agent photos of Cinderella Castle, the beach, palm trees, a setting sun, and the neon pinkness of Miami pop immediately to mind. Well, we were in Lakeland, Central Florida. Many people who aren't Detroit Tigers fans shake their heads with a look of "Huh! Never heard of it. Where is that?" and I tell them it's off of I-4, between Tampa and Orlando. Central Florida and travel-agent Florida ain't the same Florida! Our Florida gave you memories you couldn't get hanging out with Chip and Dale or Sonny Crockett and Rico Tubbs.

One Saturday (it was Florida, and because of that, I cannot remember what season it was) morning, Alisa and I boarded a van full of kids heading out to a canoe trail on the Hillsborough River in Pasco County. The Hillsborough River is pretty rustic and rich with an educational ecosystem. The ecosystem in the Hillsborough River may be fun to watch on the National Geographic Channel or to study about from a distance. But for someone like Alisa (who once decked me after I clamped down on her ankle while she was snorkeling at Clearwater Beach), facing the prospect of making herself vulnerable in a tippy canoe with such hungry creatures eyeing us is next to unlikely. But she did it. And, of course, like nineteen- to twenty-year-olds do when they see or hear of easy prey, they pick it apart (at least that was how it used to be). The talk of creepy-crawlies and toothy gators was robust en route to the river. Alisa could hardly believe she had agreed to go.

I would say there were about a dozen canoes on that trip, and she and I shared one. I was not too fond of the alligators, snapping turtles, or unforeseen creatures that may pop out of the junglelike scene that awaited us either, but I did a better job of keeping that to myself. In reality, this river is really spectacular, and those junglelike scenes are for real! Tropical forests with tangled green vegetation and tons of native Spanish moss were ever-present. With the blue sky above and the warm sun working its way through holes in the layered canopy, coupled with the quiet of only gently flowing water and a few people talking joyously, it was an encounter worth dealing with fears. In fact, there were a few times on this river that I remember thinking, *Wow! Am I really seeing this?* It was that amazing.

I assured Alisa that all would be safe, and despite the ribbing that got poured on her in the van ride there, this would be an incident-free afternoon. It was the early '90s (which now looks a bit Wild West compared to today's world), and I really think that if we were given any life jackets, they were resting on the canoe floor and certainly were not being worn. I remember thinking that I would prefer not to wear one anyway because I would rather have the ability to swim fast should the unthinkable happen.

We were on our way, paddling downstream, enjoying the day. We had taken a few snacks that were offered up before we had embarked—Snickers bars, apples, half-cut bananas—and Alisa let me don her expensive Oakley sunglasses. All was good. We did see a few of the much-heralded gators, mostly basking on the banks, plenty of giant turtles, some snakes, egrets, and heron. Our biggest threat though came from the top of the food chain: humans. Yup, my roommate Greg and his buddy, Dan, decided it would be funny to play chicken with the canoes as we rounded a bend. We did not back down. Those of you who know Alisa and/or me know if we're nothing else, we are pretty competitive (I know my cousin Vickie will laugh out loud in agreement more than anyone to this statement) even in the light of the danger. They pushed us. We got them back and shoved their canoe. Then they recovered and decided to keep it going. When they nudged us the second time, our canoe jutted to the side, headed straight for a low, over-arching branch covered with dangling moss. There was no way to evade some of that growth, and our only real opportunity to prevent capsizing was to run straight through the moss. We just had to get down as low as we could and deal with it. And we did. No big deal. We got back out in the middle of the river and began paddling again.

Then something happened that I think surprised us more than if a meteor had come crashing down in front of us: Alisa stood up—in the front of the canoe. Not only did she stand up but from my perspective behind her at the back of the small silver vessel, it appeared almost as if she were dancing. I was in shock! *What is she doing? Is what I am seeing even real?* I thought. Alisa was beating her chest and started screaming bloody murder! As if I could be more shocked, she upped the ante and (expletives removed) dove into the river. She dove into the river! Alisa dove in the river. She leaped out of the canoe and went in headfirst to the murky water filled with who knows what! This would be like someone afraid of heights leaping across a gorge—out of the blue. I can still hardly believe she did that. Now here I am, seeing her in the water and me in the rocking canoe. I did not know why she had done this. Trying to figure it all out, it suddenly became apparent. I looked under her seat, and I saw a spider the size of a star you'd put on top of a Christmas tree standing there. The thing had visible muscles. It spun around, got one look at me, and started marching down the canoe toward me! I did not want to jump in that river, but my sense of reality had just been significantly warped by seeing Alisa, the queen of not going in the river, willingly plunged in. The next thing I know, we're both in there. What a couple of chickens! Or not! We both swam to what we thought was safety—the embankment. When we simultaneously reached the muddy side, that spider's army was waiting for us as we had just entered an ambush. Getting out of the river was worse than being in the river. We retreated, if you can believe that. We opted to STAY in the water.

With much effort, Greg and Dan were able to reign in the initial perpetrator and (sorry, PETA) whack the crap out of it until it was reduced to just a massive dead flotilla. Alisa and I then hoisted ourselves back into the canoe and completed the trail. As we loaded the canoe onto the trailer rack, we did recognize that Alisa's not-so-cheap sunglasses were a victim of the day. But somehow, I still had a Snickers bar available. Let's keep it nice and say she was none too pleased with that offering/compensation!

THE GENERAL MANAGER'S SODA

"Excuse me, Mr. Gorman," one of us said (it will have been thirty years next month, so I cannot remember if it was me who had asked or if it was my buddy Jeff who initiated the action) to get the attention of then-Red Sox General Manager. Lou Gorman, who was milling about in front of the auxiliary building adjacent to the left field stands at Winter Haven's Chain O' Lakes Park that housed his spring training office in 1991. Being the gentleman he was, Mr. Gorman said hello to us and asked what he could do to help. Of course, instantaneously, Jeff and I were both like, "Uh-oh! We accomplished our goal of finding him AND getting his attention. Now talk!"

At the end of sophomore year, to satisfy his business class's monster project that had been sitting on the syllabus since January, Jeff was required to interview the manager of an organization. Though I did not share this class with Jeff, I still thought I could contribute. I told Jeff he ought to think bigger and take advantage of what may exist beyond the one-mile radius surrounding our school's campus. Naturally, my first thought was to get over to Winter Haven, which was maybe twenty miles to our east, to see what we could muster up with the Sox. Why not? Jeff, who hailed from a little New Jersey hamlet just the other side of the Del Water Gap and was a longtime Toronto Blue Jays fan, loved baseball as much as I did, and after all, he was the one with the car, and I had no other way to get there anyway.

After we composed ourselves and explained what was needed, Lou Gorman agreed to a sit-down interview, and we scheduled something with him for the following week. Of course, our roster grew. Now Jeff and his classmate, Brian, a Rhode Islander who also had to complete the same assignment, joined our other friend, Jeff, a

Connecticut kid who was always worth having around, and me. We made up a solid foursome that the Farrelly brothers would have enjoyed had they been writing comedy at that early point.

Between the day we made the request and the day we went to the interview, the four of us scrambled to put together something that resembled suits (I am glad no pictures exist). We borrowed shoes and ties and jackets and somehow made ourselves look quite presentable for the BIG DAY. Tic Tacs and Mentos were flowing on the car ride to the Sox complex. I think we were all getting kind of nervous, rehearsing who might say what when we arrived, as we got closer. At the time, this was a pretty big deal to all of us. At least in the Boston market, Lou Gorman was a pretty familiar face. Anytime a Boston player's contract was disputed, or a new free agent signing happened over the winter, New Englanders everywhere would see Lou explaining the process of how the transaction unfolded and what the move meant to the team. He was also a big man with a large head and a big presence, so to have him to ourselves for maybe an hour or so was almost too good to be true. But it was true. And here we were. Our time to be adults was upon us.

Lou took us to the small makeshift conference room. He sat at the head of the long table, which consumed much of the available space. Jeff, the Jeff whose class this was and who drove us here, and Brian sat on either side of the table but closest to Lou. Naturally, they were here for a reason. Then the other Jeff and I sat across from each other, two seats away from Lou. (We pitched it to him that we were all doing this for school. I didn't feel bad about that white lie because after all, what is college if not a ground from which to learn, and is not interviewing an excellent skill to practice?) For the first time, the four of us were now forced to quietly look at each other. Seeing my buddies in suits and all being so stoic was like watching an ape drive a car to go to church. We all knew how comical but deadly serious this moment was to us. I am not sure if I have ever wanted to burst out laughing—and didn't—more than I did this day.

Lou didn't help our situation, and he really tested us. He started the "interview" by giving us a rundown of his storied career (Google it. It's long). Between the recalled episodes of his time in the game, he would pause—and I mean pause. Lou stalled a few times for what seemed like twenty to thirty seconds. In those horrific pauses, he would look straight forward and close his eyes and stop talking. Now we're still trying to tiptoe past the fine line of being teenagers and being mature for maybe the first time ever and definitely for the first time in a collaborative setting. Our discomfort led to brief thoughts of terror: *What if Lou passes while we are interviewing him?* Finally, Mr. Gorman wrapped up his monologue and decided he could use a little pick-me-up. He gathered the most enormous cup I had ever seen to that point, filled it with large ice cubes, and poured the rest of his two-liter bottle of Diet Coke to the absolute brim. Being the gentleman that he was, Lou offered each of us some. Of course, none of us knew the etiquette of such an exchange. We all declined for the sake of staying on the safe side of doing the right thing.

Thinking I was smart and wanted to help my buddies by throwing the first rock on the ice, I wisely asked him about his thoughts of the Cubs' signing of the second baseman Ryne Sandberg, which had just happened the day before. *Question one of many*, I thought. This was our time to pick the brain of someone "in the know." This was going to be good. I can't believe I had just mustered up the guts to keep myself together enough to ask such a baseball-important and seemingly poignant question. Wow. Maybe I do have it in me to do more… Perhaps I will be successful in my postcollege career. Good stuff! Well, I don't recall what Lou ever said about Sandberg, and I am sure Brian and the two Jeffs don't either. What happened next was so unexpected that I am not sure if it was a wonderful learning experience (as in "we're all just human") or so shocking that I almost erased it from my memory.

As soon as I asked my sharp-witted question, Lou paused as if to hear me out and then think of a solid response. The four of us simultaneously inhaled as we knew the first milestone was met, and now we were about to relax and allow the conversation to unfold. Then Lou swung his big right arm out as he began to speak. He backhanded that enormous container that was his cup of Diet Coke. Twenty-five ice cubes shot across the table in all directions. Brian, a member of the school's track team and arguably the most athletic of us all, immediately shot out of his seat. Obviously, he either owned much of his own suit or could not afford the price of dry cleaning before returning its parts to the different people from whom he borrowed it, and whatever nervousness and sense of stoicism he was employing went down the toilet. The Jeffs and I got Diet Coke all over our laps. We really didn't know what to do now in this situation. Handling the bloopers of the interviewee is not discussed in any class I have ever known. Swear to God, Lou looked around as calmly as could be, like what just happened never happened. He had one ply of Bounty, the "quicker picker upper," on a roll in that room. One ply—the one that is glued to the brown part. Of course, he tried to use that, but it looked like he was trying to dry up a tub of water with one washcloth. So he took the brown roll itself and just starts squeegeeing the remaining liter of soda and dozens of ice cubes onto the carpeted floor. *This is just too much! Lou, you're killing us! We've been holding nervous energy for an hour, and now you do this to us? Is this even real?* we all thought.

Rest in Peace, Mr. Gorman. Thank God you briefly left that room to search for more towels because there was just no way Jeff and Brian could have completed that assignment if we didn't get the chance to explode when you stepped away for a moment.

EIGHTY-TWO ORANGES

In the early spring at my Florida college campus, the science department's orange trees came into full bloom. The campus was known for vacating on weekends, and I, a New Englander without transportation and little money, was stuck in my dorm room, often alone and hungry at night. One Saturday night, under cover of darkness, I took a brown paper grocery bag, walked over to the west side of campus where the sweetest aroma of citrus awaited, bypassed the Do Not Touch signs and proceeded to fill the bag with numerous orange spheres of deliciousness.

Upon returning to my dorm, I dumped the bag out and counted how many I had collected. Eighty-two! Eighty-two tree-to-dorm fruits from the gods. On Sunday, I sat to write a paper and lined up a handful of them next to me. Within minutes, ten were gone. I couldn't stop there. I continued eating them—ten at a time. Ten! Ten whole oranges, one right after the other. Their sweetness has been something I have never been able to replicate and would fail to describe accurately, so I won't even try. That day, when I threw the empty brown bag in the trash, I had consumed over four thousand milligrams of Vitamin C. I haven't been sick since.

SECTION 6

SINGLE DAYS

Being a single adult for a decade plus was no joy ride for me in the 1990s into the 2000s. I am sure it did not appear as painful as it felt at times. There was plenty of loneliness and little money. I recognized my situation as it was happening and realized that there was no proven avenue of quick change. I provided all sorts of experiences for myself. I held dozens of jobs and moved around freely. I stayed in good shape—playing organized baseball, running several marathons, and was never a stranger to the pickup basketball scene. I met many terrific people and got to see the world from exciting angles. It was a good time. Sometimes I miss it, and I would have to think hard if I would want to trade it for anything else. Since I can't change it, I will choose to own it.

THE BRAINTREE SPLIT

One summer, a couple of years after graduating from college, I stayed in Brockton with my aunt and uncle in what had been my grandparents' house. At the time, they had three young daughters (my cousins) ranging in age from about eleven to two years old. I spent a lot of my time at work then but would see the kids in the afternoon and evening. It was a pleasant experience—they seemed to enjoy me, and I enjoyed them. I unquestionably recognized that I was in a role-model sort of position. That was fine, but one day, a challenge presented itself to that title.

I was driving my twelve-tone red/brown/gray/rusted flavor-of-the-year hooptie through Boston, snaking my way over toward Mass. Ave. so I could head back to South Shore, Brockton. I was in the middle lane of Herald Street when the right I needed to take for Harrison popped up on me much faster than I had been anticipating. A quick look through both the side and rearview mirrors indicated an abrupt turn would be okay to take, albeit borderline illegal in the approach. Well, what to my wondering eyes would appear but a silver SUV—straight outta nowhere—in the right lane. I completely cut off this vehicle. No doubt about it. My fault—100 percent! Luckily though, the driver was aware and swerved to avoid me and was able to continue traveling down Herald.

When I got to the end of Harrison, at Mass. Ave., where I was going to go left to head to the Southeast Expressway, guess what? There was the silver SUV right behind me (and I mean right behind) from a distance we may have appeared hitched. It was a young couple around my age, a man driving and a woman on the passenger side, and they were ready to kill someone! Me! I don't know if I have ever seen a couple (I assume they were a couple—a couple people anyway) so mad, for the same reason and on the same page, at someone else as they were with me. My observations of them came via the mirror that had failed to capture their reflection a mile back.

I recall they had a Bruins license plate border and Mass plates, of course. The woman, especially, was LOSING HER MIND—pointing, screaming, dropping f-bomb after f-bomb, beet-red in the face. Well, *Stay calm*, I thought. I never let them know I saw them. I turned left when the light turned green, went under the City Hospital, made another left to the Expressway, passed the jail and then right onto the Expressway. They turned left, went under the City Hospital, made another left, went by the prison, and right onto the Expressway. We approached 93 like Ponch and John from *CHiPs*, only not on motorcycles. Keeping up the appearance (and not giving them an ounce of satisfaction), I gave them no reason to believe I ever knew they were there. I drifted around cars, from the right lane to the middle lane to the left lane. No blinker. Just zigzagging away. I had one hand on the wheel and the other tapping on the roof to some Hootie & the Blowfish or Dave Matthews Band on ZLX or BCN on Mix 98.5. I made it look like I was enjoying the warm summer day, cruising along. But the SUV matched me lane for lane, from right to left and back again. I slyly kept them in my vision the whole time.

Boston to Milton to Quincy, now halfway to Brockton, this guy was on a mission. I was starting to worry. I could not bring this scene to the house, in front of the kids. I was quickly beginning to run out of time, and I had to think of something. Pulling over and talking to them was out of the question. It was a rarity, but I had a full tank of gas. I thought, *Well if I need to, I could make it to New York.* Then maybe it was the spirits of my ancestors, buried on either side of this highway, that lent me a gusto of energy and some clear thinking. *This is my home field. I have been on this expressway, in this exact area, hundreds of times since I was born.* So I gathered a great idea. I separated myself from other cars (except them, of course; now they were doing me a favor in this quick-thinking scheme).

I got to what is called the Braintree Split, where you can take Route 3 to the Cape or get on Route 24 and head to Brockton/Taunton/Providence, Rhode Island. I wanted 24, but they didn't need to know that. So I got on the left side and started heading for the Cape. They got on the left and also headed for the Cape. Checking mirrors, checking mirrors, checking mirrors! I was getting excited to pull this off. My heart was beating faster, but now with joy and no longer with fear. And boom, you could fit a credit card between my driver's side front quarter panel and those orange sand-filled barrels that split the highway. My SUV friends were way too close to me to react fast enough to my maneuver. To the Cape they went. Finally, after miles of feigning aloofness, I glared over at them, locked eyes, and pointed to the sky with finger number two.

BLEDSOE ON THE GREEN LINE

It was a Friday afternoon at the beginning of the fall, some twenty-three years ago. I took the Green Line from Needham back into the city en route to my apartment in Dorchester. The train was quite empty when I got on it. I would never take a seat because the minute I did, every pregnant woman with two kids and a stroller in the metro area would get on, and I didn't care to be caught in the limelight, which came with offering up a seat. But then, if I didn't, I hated the feeling of guilt that would then envelope me. So I would usually become a "door standee," probably appearing to some like I may be a hired train bouncer, deciding when I will move to allow others off. But this day, I just thought, *Screw it. I want to sit down. It has been a long week. I'm tired. I hate my job. I walked a mile to get to the train. I'm sitting.*" So I did.

The green line then had forward-facing seats, two together on each side of a center aisle. Lo and behold, the then-Patriots quarterback, Drew Bledsoe, was there. He had his blue practice jersey on with that plain white number eleven across the front of it. I remember the green trees right behind him. There he is. There I am—just Drew Bledsoe and me. In fact, he's throwing me a pass. It's high and to my left. I got a shot at it though. I reached. I threw out a good sports grunt as I gave my all for an opportunity to bring in this tight spiral from his cannon-like arm. Nanoseconds before feeling that slick leather sting my fingertips, I realized a pretty girl was sitting in the seat right next to me, now under the pit of my outstretched left arm.

Oh shit! So quickly, my NFL dream was instantly replaced by sheer terror as I realized I just jumped up, screamed on an otherwise quiet but now-packed Friday afternoon trolley and lunged heartily for a ball only I saw. *You gotta be kidding! Was Bledsoe a dream? I just f——ing jumped up and yelled? Oh my god! I'm taking this (expletive) all the way to the red line transfer too,* I thought to myself. And trying to get off that jammed sardine can before Park Street practically required a preregistration sign-up sheet in the late '90s. I don't remember how hard I peered out that side window for the duration of my trip, but there just may still be two burn holes on the right-side window of MBTA car 2881.

MERRY KOREASTMAS!

My apartment was nestled in the Pa Dong section of the city, essentially an offshoot of Taegu formed by a valley. It did not take much effort to get away from the crowds of people and be up into the wooded hillside, where the vistas were magnificent, displaying images of a prospering Asian city. Taegu offered signature tall white apartment complexes and the numerous external cranes dotting the different construction projects throughout the third most populous metropolis on the peninsula, south of the 38th parallel. The air was so uniquely refreshing there that whenever I have been in anything similar since, I would tell whoever I am with that "right now reminds me of being in Korea." I had been in Korea for a month. I would be away from home on Christmas for the first time.

Christmas was a big deal to my family and to me. We always made it grand. My earliest memory in life, in fact, was visiting the popular Enchanted Village at Jordan Marsh in Boston's Downtown Crossing when I was probably just old enough to walk. We always visited Santa, got a real tree, decorated the house—inside and out—and would rip red and green construction paper rings each day, leading up to the twenty-fifth. My sister and I would plan our early December weeks around the TV holiday specials. "Rudolph's on, on Tuesday. Eat supper early!" If you miss it, you don't get to see it again until you're another year older. There was no taping or recording these shows then. There were no VHS or DVD options even. One and done! You dealt with the Peter Paul Almond Joy commercials and watched Ronald McDonald float some kid around on his shoulders on some frozen pond in between when Rudolph finds Yukon Cornelius, and they get to the Island of Misfit Toys. I can still recite the lines to this day. *Frosty*, *'Twas the Night Before Christmas* (the one where the mouse breaks that town clock), *The Grinch* (the cartoon one, with the pink sky), *Charlie Brown* (we NEVER called it Peanuts, by the way), all of 'em. Loved 'em. There's something about only getting to see something once, then having to wait. The pain of missing it or waiting for it makes the memory of it more tremendous! (If I only learned that before I was forty-five!)

When the big day finally approached, we would make a birthday cake for Jesus, get all sorts of deli meat and finger rolls (FINGAH rolls, kid!), and joyfully head to church for Christmas Eve Mass. Mass! Was there ever a better time to go to Mass than on Christmas Eve? I mean, if you're ever going to go, Christmas Eve is the time to be there! We went to Mass every Sunday though. So my mother would always mutter something about the ones who would come just this once a year (or that and Easter, she'd say) and take our seats. In those days, families had unwritten dedicated pews. Ours was the fourth or fifth row back on the far right side. Never did we sit on the left. (This might have been because we were never there on time and because we would have to park on the street because the lot was always packed. Then we would stroll in the moment the congregation would stand up to recite one of those weekly prayers. We used the crowd as a smoke screen. As soon as everyone would sit back down upon the priest's gesture, suddenly, the White family was among the populous. My mother had this down to a tee.) The whole time you'd be at church though, after imagining why someone might walk so far just to give someone else a package of frankincense, all you could think was, *We better hurry up and get outta here! You said Santa was already in China, and that was well before we even got dressed for this!* It was like you must have felt like Paul Revere had felt, knowing somewhere out there in the darkness, those Brits were creepin' in! He could almost hear them from out on the ocean. I could feel Santa getting closer.

All right, all right, all right, I'd think (and unquestionably demonstrated in the form of body language) from ages five through probably later than I would have liked any girl I was ever interested in to know. I'd go on with my thoughts: *It's Thursday night. In reality, I know it's Christmas Eve, which never feels like any day—it's too special to be called any day of the week—but do we really need to go up for the host? Today? We just did that Sunday! Come on! If we are not in bed soon, we are screwed! Let's go!*

A little "Hark! The Herald Angels Sing" and "Silent Night" later, and we would be back out in our parents' freezer of a car, looking nervously up in the winter sky for a glimmer of red. You kinda wanted to see the big guy and his boys up there, but not really at the same time! You know what I mean? It's a weird mix. So now, in Korea, I am this adult, unmarried and alone in a foreign country. I had just accepted a position as an English teacher, on a whim, after having answered an ad in the *Boston Globe* classifieds just two months prior. I went this route because no work had ever appealed to me, and the itch to escape Dodge had become a full-fledged rash. Maybe when I took the job, my foreshadowing superpower was down, and I hadn't factored in missing Christmas, but nonetheless, there was nothing I could do about this in 1996, and I had to deal with the consequences of the decision I had made. Christmas would be just me (and a fellow teacher/roommate)!

With this mid-90s yuletide ("Siri: what does 'yuletide' mean?") upon me, I could not just do nothing though. Serendipitously, on a hike right after Thanksgiving, I had come across this solitary green tree—one of its kind and the only one even close to resembling a Christmas tree that I witnessed in my time in Korea. It was almost as if the Ghost of Christmas Past put that fledgling fir there for me, not even far from my little spot. Immediately, I knew what that needled conifer's fate would be. There would be a Christmas after all, and I would have a tree to prove it. But though my Yuletide idol, Clark Griswold, was able to yank a much bigger version out of the Chicagoland ground just a few years earlier on the silver screen, I had to be crafty about separating this living being from the same earth. For all I knew, I may have been on Hill 303 from the gruesome battle forty-six years before, and this would require wit and courage.

The Koreans have this exciting tradition in which they will bury certain family members on the sides of hills, often facing the sun. They clear out patches of land in areas that are not exactly easy to get to and at places where I cannot believe Americans would ever attempt to recreate. On a different hike on another day a few weeks prior, I had come across a pretty new burial site. So fresh, in fact, that the handsaw used to clear the plot was still there. At first, the saw looked like a long, thin instrument covered in a rigid plastic green sheath. It was about two feet long and had a slight curve to it, with sharp teeth that made it the perfect tool for the eldest child to practice his due diligence upon the death (and burial ceremony) of an ancestor. At second thought, with a golden light coming down upon it from the heavens, this American hill climber recognized that this cutting instrument had not yet seen its last duty. This saw was the gift that would keep on giving! Far from being done—once cast aside as a relic upon a sacred mound—this particular saw had at least one more purpose left in it. Well, not to be an ass, I respectfully stood silent, facing the recently deceased man's tomb, and gently requested permission to borrow his son's saw. I didn't hear a no, and so I proceeded to take it and move along. I did explain to the man, who wouldn't be celebrating his first Christmas in several decades (if he celebrated Christmas), that having a tree would mean the world to me and that one saw could bind two traditions. How cool!

Problem: the tree I spotted was on the east hill of the valley, and the burial plot ("home of the saw") was on the west. In between was a fairly dried-up, albeit rocky, riverbed, and many, many houses and lots of people, none of whom were American people with blond hair wearing a Red Sox cap. So when I got closer to the residential area, the saw seemed more like a giant sword, and it could not be seen in public and most definitely not in the hands of the person typing this in 2020. With practically no choice but still driven to accomplish this mission of preventing twenty-five years of an annual tree-hoisting tradition from snapping, the saw-now-sword made its way down the outside of my right pant leg. It pretty much took up every inch of the distance between my hip and my ankle, and I was able to secure it by continuously holding its handle against me. This may sound kind of convenient, but the natural bending of our knees and the sight of this alien not letting go of his side was loudly curious, if nothing else. Not being one for the limelight, the walk through the village suddenly seemed almost like walking from Seoul to Pusan.

One slip of the hand, and that saw was coming through the bottom of those pants. So my palm had to stay in place. Then, for some reason, unless put into certain predicaments, you don't always notice particular things until a situation presents itself. For example, where did this ten-foot-high concrete wall at the edge of that said riverbed come from? I don't really remember it. I must have scaled down it en route to the hill with the saw, but now that I have to climb up it without bending my knee, it was as if the damn thing had been put in place by the enemies to the North in an attempt to stop this American descendent from marching on while I was hiking that day.

With care and discomfort (on the inside and out), I captured the tree and hid it in a spot where I could come find it later, when I could use the cover of darkness. (If the sword in my pants wasn't bad enough, carrying a small tree on my shoulder was over-the-top.) With the cut complete, I quickly retraced my steps back up to the burial site, and with tremendous relief, I returned the great man's tool. My heart returned to its regular rate. Later that night, I completed the mission and erected the magnificent little tree atop a small table in my apartment. Months later, when I explained my story to my class of Korean women, they were aghast, laughing nervously and uncontrollably, and they told me I needed to replace that tree. I said I would, but I still haven't. The years are pinging by, and I do not have plans at this time to return to South Korea. Uh-oh. Anyone going over there any time in the next few years? Let me know. I have a packet of seeds I need to give you. Until then, I hope this story can act as a virtual placeholder for the life of that tree. Merry Christmas, everybody!

RIDING IN A PONY

I was always searching for odd jobs to string together a substantive life as a guy in his midtwenties living in the greater New York City area while holding out for that great discovery of getting the proverbial break that I would consider desirable. I spent eighteen months living there. Actually, I lived in Jersey City, right across the Hudson River from the World Trade Center and a handful of blocks from the shore of which the ferries to Ellis Island dock. Often, I would peruse the *Sunday Times* for employment opportunities and one time found one of interest: driver / tour guide for pedicabs of New York. The old rickshaw idea was upgrading to a new industry in the city at that time in pedicabs, which are essentially bike-led carriages used for luxury purposes and touring popular areas and attractions. People would pay for a tour. Instead of having one of those iconic Central Park horses draw them around the sights and sounds of the midtown green space, pedicabs have a human being replacing the horse and generating momentum via a bike.

The ad said that no experience was necessary but that you had to have good character, be comfortable in busy locations, and be physically capable of handling a certain amount of weight. I felt I possessed those qualities, so I inquired. I was invited to visit George, the owner of PONY, which at the time was just a tick past a start-up, that following Sunday. We met at his location in Downtown Manhattan. George had a handful of pedicabs there, in an old refurbished garage with an attached paved lot. His place seemed really cool—a century-old red brick building which had probably stood as a warehouse of sorts for decades of its existence but spacious enough now to store the PONY buggies and with several workbenches with which to perform minor maintenance. George had great music playing and really customized his spot to make it seem like an enjoyable space to spend your day at work. Greater even, George had his dog, Trixie, there hanging out with him. From first impressions, I was all about this place and figured I could quickly get used to this style of living, err working.

In that paved lot, George had a system of cones set up. I don't know if he quickly had put them out there before I arrived or if this setup was always in place. Would there be others, like me, coming here today to see about this *Times*-listed job? I mean, after all, the *New York Times* is not a small paper, and those ads can't be cheap. I found it both unusual and relieving that I was the only person to meet the owner (and his dog). Maybe this meant I had a pretty good shot of getting offered some hours. I undoubtedly had hoped so.

After we exchanged niceties and talked for a bit, George wanted me to show him what I could do. I got on the bike—pedicab empty—and whirled around the cones like it was nobody's business. Easy peasy! Then George and Trixie, a sweet German shepherd-lab mix, hopped in the back to "make it more realistic" weight-wise. Same cones. Same good job. George even told me he was kind of impressed with how quickly I took to my potentially new profession. Enough of the child's play, George wanted to see this prospect perform on the bigger stage. To the streets we went. Frank Sinatra crooned that New York may be the city that never sleeps, and while that may have some truth to it if you are ever going to find the Big Apple at least sluggish, it is on Sunday.

A sluggish New York still made other major US metropolitan areas I have visited—Minneapolis, Houston, San Diego, Seattle, to name a few—seem small. For some reason, when I got onto Broadway, I started feeling somewhat overwhelmed. Broadway, where the lights are bright and which is the much-heralded destination of phenomenal actors, theater fans, and tourists worldwide, was where I had my little tryout. By sight alone, they were a bit of a spectacle. If I try to resist anything in life, it is being at the center of an eyesore. Plus, we seemed to have full access to the streets, like any other motorized vehicle, which meant I could navigate through any of the three available lanes. George must have trusted me as we waited no time at all to get right into the thick of things. We crossed Houston Street, then Canal Street—two of the biggest East-West thoroughfares in Lower Manhattan, but not without me making my shiny star fall several notches. Approaching both intersections, I was more preoccupied with stopping at the light and preserving the lives of George, Trixie, and myself as real cabs and other cars zoomed past and around me. In doing so, I failed to appropriately downshift the bike, which translated into very slow and challenging starts when the light went green. This was highly frowned upon by the motorists behind me—and George. The New York drivers had little tolerance for this goofy-looking gadget, and I could hear George sigh.

I turned behind me and muttered something to George that indicated a promise to downshift next time. He made other plans. Instead of the big streets, George directed me to meander over toward the lesser Lafayette Street. Who knows, but maybe he was thinking we jumped in a little too deep too soon. I doubt the average driver or pedestrian of a city may realize that most streets have a pitch to them, or I should say a crown. By that, I mean to say the center of a roadway is often slightly higher than its sides—like a sports field. This allows for runoff and reduces the risk of flooding. But on this damn pedicab, that crown grew increasingly evident and became a nemesis of this new driver as it constantly tried to force the bike and carriage off to the edge. My left forearm, I recall, was getting exhausted. Only sheer will and the determination not to be embarrassed allowed me to forge through the burn happening inside the antebrachium leftus. Will and determination be fooled; the burn began to own me. The ole boy here went just a few feet too far in overcompensation. Then to the bewilderment of yours truly, and indeed to the business owner, our little bicycle/pedicab combo nailed the granite curb on the left side of the street. It landed in a purely perpendicular formation—absolutely head-on—creating a perfect right angle!

The maneuver cost me the job. George and I both knew it. We mutually and silently agreed that this opportunity would not be for me—no need to actually really even talk about it. I could take the loss. George seemed to be kind and fair: he did not make a big deal about it, and I appreciated that. But only one thing stood between this incident and ending our relationship, and that was returning to his garage. When I think about it, I am not sure which part is worse: the feeling of losing control of this guy's custom-made pedicab (with him present) and failing to get a job or what happened after.

George insisted on riding us home. I conceded and sat in the back with Trixie. I have been in some awkward situations in life, but this one kind of stands alone. Even when I hear the word "awkward," I imagine the smell of Trixie's breath and can feel the breeze of the wind as it hurried past the back seat of the carriage, cooling my blushed face.

SPACE HEATERS AND HYDROFOILS

It wasn't until I got to Korea that I understood that to remain there at my new teaching position, I would need to leave the peninsula and go to a consulate in another nation to get approved to stay. What a racket (IMHO). Anyway, the easiest way to accomplish this was to head over to Japan, and at least at that time (December 1996), the best location for completing what I needed was in Osaka. To get to Japan quickly and affordably, I took a hydrofoil—a slick catamaran that slalomed some Korean islands and then rose up and blasted across the Sea of Japan—from Pusan to Fukuoka.

Though that was a great experience, this many years later, what I remember most about it all was waiting for the departure and sitting in a Wendy's restaurant near the hydrofoil dock in Pusan's port area. (This story always reminded me that this might not be something you would see in America, even though it was at Wendy's. Dave Thomas, did you even know about this location?) Being a cold winter day, Wendy's had a space heater parked right in the middle of the seating area. The heater was attached to an extension cord that was plugged into an outlet on the ceiling. It worked well...until it didn't. One minute, the heater was a blessing, but then, out of nowhere, the wire began sparking and even got so frayed that it started to separate from the back of the mechanism. The sparking increased and drew everyone's attention. (Here comes the this-is-not-America part). A Wendy's worker, I would say a male about fifteen to seventeen years old, came over with a pair of scissors and approached the situation with guile and determination. Regardless of our language barrier, I could not help but yell out, "Nooo!"

The kid then cut the wire (still plugged in). No recourse. Nothing bad happened. I was surprised (I would have written *shocked*, but I didn't want to be confusing here). I still wonder why he didn't get hurt, and everything turned out okay. I would definitely not try that. I did not expect that outcome. I think I was left saying to myself, "Okay. Okay. Huh!" and shaking my head. Sometimes, you just don't know. (How have I been stung by a dead bee before, and this kid cut a live wire with scissors, then just calmly returned to the Frosty machine?)

THE REST AREA TREE

My eyes were getting heavy, and the hash marks on 495 were starting to blur and merge. I had to get off the road. I stopped at the next rest area and parked in a well-lit area, near the entrance to the restrooms, underneath a tree. I put the seat back and told myself, "Try to sleep for fifteen minutes and then let's get back on the road." I dozed off with no problem.

Before I knew it, I was driving again, back on that same stretch of highway in northwestern metro Boston. "OH MY GOD," I screamed! I shot up and slammed on the brakes to avoid the tree right in front of my speeding hood. "HOLY ——! BLEEPEDETY BLEEP! WHAT THE BLEEP!" Probably white as a ghost and feeling bloodless, I can only imagine what the people parked in the car next to me thought.

HAVE PENCIL AND NOTEBOOK AND THE MCDONALD'S PAY PHONE

A lot of you have been fortunate enough to participate in some sort of athletics at the high school—or higher—level, and, no doubt, it was always a delight to pick up a copy of the local newspaper to see your name mentioned. If not just you, your family and neighbors were also proud to see your name in print. I recall the thrill myself of picking up a copy of the *Portsmouth Herald* one afternoon only to find a photo of me pitching in a winning effort in the previous night's American Legion baseball game at Leary Field. I was elated.

Years later, both in college, when I studied journalism and post-graduation, when I supplemented my income with some local writing gigs, I covered prep sports for the Lakeland Ledger and then *Foster's Daily Democrat* (Dover, New Hampshire) and the *Patriot Ledger* (Quincy, Massachusetts), respectively. When I was assigned a game, most typically Friday night football, I had three goals in each article: (1) Be accurate. (The game details had to be correct, and there should be no misspellings, for the love of God. There is no letdown like playing your heart out only to have some no-name writer botch your last name in tomorrow's paper); (2) Include as many worthy kids' names as possible. (After all, that is what everyone who participated is ultimately looking for anyway. Let's be honest. So when a kid wearing number sixty-four, who plays four years of varsity and never once touches the ball and probably never received a mention in the paper before, makes a crucial play that allows something to happen, I got that kid in there, one way or another); and (3) I tried to write an opening line that would entice any reader, from the excited parent to the pedestrian townie who may only typically peruse the headlines of anything less than college or pro sports, to read at least into the second paragraph.

Unless you belong to the micro-society of folks who have ever been paid to attend, chart, and describe a local high school game, in all sorts of weather conditions and with a one-hour deadline, you may have no idea how a story germinates from field to print. In the mid-1990s, there were no laptops, no cell phones, no access to much other than a pencil, a notebook, a program, a local payphone…, and a ticking clock. So I will share.

So many fields, so many towns. York, Scarborough, Abington, Chestnut Hill, Bartow, Tampa, Winter Haven, Needham, Plymouth, Brockton, Auburndale, Kennebunk, Newton, Lake Wales, Whitman, Randolph, Somersworth, on and on and on. Many of these locations were not so easy to find, especially in the more rural areas and after daylight saving time had expired. Once at the site, I would have to prove I was not just a fan trying to evade the $3 ticket price and somehow obtain a program as a compliment. Worse sometimes was broaching the press box and throwing the uncomfortable wrench in what seemed like a tight fraternity's weekly clubhouse conclave. No doubt, each week, I was "the new guy."

I scrambled to keep up with the play on the field and utilized a self-derived graphing system with symbol usage—and didn't eat or drink one thing (and definitely not using the restroom—where were those?). I would grab a few loose and predictable quotes from each coach and bound off to my car, which was often down some dimly lit side street. I had nowhere to go to write and only an hour to get a story together. Too many times, my thumbs were so damn cold I could barely clutch a pencil unless I held my hands over the dashboard heater for at least ten minutes. I would typically find the nearest McDonald's parking lot and utilize their exterior illumination and, once ready, their serviceable pay phone. I sat in the car and counted up the stats and pasted together the story of each drive that mattered most. From there, in the near-dark and now-blazing hot car, I would tie things up with quasi-notes that sounded like a written story and then head to the phone with my notebook open to the page with the cleanest story line. I would call collect into the office and get one of the editors on the line. With eyes squinting and trying to talk slowly enough for my dictation to make sense—stopping to ensure quotations were placed correctly and so forth—I would flip through three or four pages with my non-phone hand and talk my way through the game.

I didn't make much money, and I thought it might be a career I would want to pursue there for a bit, but there was always that slight fulfillment that arrived the following day when you opened the paper and found your name (or your child's or teammate's or neighbor's name) in type. I hope the kids who played appreciated seeing their hard work pay off in the form of publicized recognition. I hope the parents look back fondly with proud memories and have held onto yellowed cutout pieces including their baby's progress and on-field achievements. I hope everyone else now has a better understanding and increased admiration of the work it took (and still takes, despite the advent of all sorts of technology) to make that all happen.

GLIDER RIDER

Have you ever been in a glider? Not that I ask that often, but when I do, I have yet to run into anyone who ever says yes (I am sure I will now, of course, because I put this out there). One time I got myself into a situation, and it included me being in a glider—yes, the engineless flying contraption/plane. So let me tell you how it is, at least from my perspective.

It was 1997, and I had planned to go tandem skydiving with my buddy Dave. Among a few others, we invited my uncle to join us. At that time, my uncle was still a driver for BFI, the then-big waste management company in Boston. With him, he brought another guy—an older gentleman who, like my uncle, was a veteran and fellow marine and fellow BFI worker.

We all met up at Skydive Pepperell, north of Boston—kinda near Nashua, New Hampshire. Because of morning winds that day, our dive times were delayed and put in jeopardy of being canceled. Because of that, a bunch of us were stranded in the lobby area of the facility. My uncle's buddy, who happened to be sitting just to my right and was clearly struggling to read his waiver/release form—his eyes just "ain't like they used to be," he had told me. So doing what anyone would do, I helped him out. I took his clipboard and filled out the form for him. He was pretty appreciative, and as we got to talking, he asked me: "Hey, have you ever been up in a glider?" Of course, I hadn't. "How about I pay for you to go on a glider ride while we all wait here?" he offered in exchange for having been helpful to him.

"For real? Sure! Why not?" I replied.

Off to the side of the airport, which Skydive Pepperell uses, is a bevy of hangars, storing a handful of gliders along with some other smaller prop planes. For $75, anyone could pay for a glider ride. He paid, and so I went. A glider ride is like nothing I had ever experienced. First of all, I met the pilot, Steve, on the tarmac. He asked me to help him push the glider onto the runway. Yup—push! The thing was pretty light for a plane. There were two in-line seats in the cockpit—one in front of the other. I got to sit in front. We linked up to a towplane with what looked like your typical True Value hardware-purchased yellow-and-black nylon rope. Once the towplane began to move, so did we—immediately, I had memories rush in from days of childhood when we'd rig up a big wheel with a radio flyer and construct some sort of makeshift train system around the driveway/neighborhood. That's how the initial grab of the towline felt in the glider. Anyway, finally, we got up to an altitude that sat well with Steve. He instructed me to pull the release knob, which untethered the towline and set us totally free.

With the prop plane now gone, the glider fell silent. The only sound similar to this which I have experienced and could compare is when I would be on a smaller boat deep-sea fishing when there is no land in sight, and the engine is cut off. Only a rhythm of gentle creeks and loud deafness fills the air. In fact, I have found the sound of those creeks unsettling, almost nauseating, instead of peaceful or relaxing. To me, whether in a vulnerable seafaring vessel or in a powerless glider, creeks reinforce fragility and physical closeness to tragedy.

Steve let us drift around for a few minutes. It was beautiful, but I only could think, *Later today, I need to go up even higher than this and jump! Oh my god! What am I doing?*

Steve inquired from his back seat perch: "So did you want mild or wild today?" Now what twentysomething guy is going to say "mild" when there is only one other dude there (and I didn't know him)? Wild it was, I notified Steve. Wow. And was it ever! Immediately after my verbal confirmation, Steve ordered me to grab the control stick. I did. Then he told me to dip the "starboard" (right to most of us) wing down. *Yeah, right,* I thought. Like a wet noodle, my "pull" into a dip barely registered as a movement of any kind. (Listen up, sitting here at my dining room table in 2021, I have zero problems mimicking a glider control stick dip to the right—or left—but let's just say it's a lot easier saying it now than doing it then. Know what I mean?) Steve took over, and did he ever show me what a "wild dip" looked like. Dear God! Both sides too. When that was done, Steve informed me he was just warming up! Yup!

As the glider slowly descended to the earth's outer crust—doing what gliders do—Steve pulled us into some end-around upside-down loop. To do so, and I recall Steve's scientific explanation, "We dropped altitude to increase velocity." Wow! The loop started by him pointing that glider absolutely straight down. We were cruising, like a lawn dart falling to its plastic circular target. Then he yanked us completely up and backward. Contents resting on the floorboards were instantaneously shifted to the glass bubble in a clang of harmony. I remember seeing a dime fall by my head and settle momentarily on the glass—below my now-inverted position. I am pretty sure Steve and I had worn helmets, and I feel like I must have looked like *Dumb and Dumber's* Lloyd Christmas on a scooter or Chris Farley in his Whale Boy sketch.

The world kinda never looked the same after that loop. It really didn't! Before long, we had run out of height and had to land, which we did, but in the grass near the runway (I never asked why that approach was like it was, but I figure some things are just better left unsaid). Maybe gliders always land in the grass. If you had asked me then if I could go back to filling out that guy's waiver form, I might have said I would probably have wished I had not sat near him. But now I think that was one of the best things I ever got to do!

GUMP WITH RICE

Last week, my buddy Mike from Connecticut suggested that my stories are like something from *Forrest Gump*. This morning, I started laughing when this memory hit me. This one makes me think Mike is not incorrect.

While working the grounds at Fenway Park in the baseball off-season, we would undoubtedly get laid off. Then, of course, it was time to find winter work. What would any single due in Massachusetts, with access to some wheels, think would be a good option? You got it! In 1998, I got hired by the New England Patriots to work that season with the Foxboro Stadium ground crew. Why not? Right?

Gump moment: During the Pats' games, we would stand behind the South End Zone, in that corner without seats which we used to get to Gator and other equipment on and off the field during the rest of the week. One Sunday, the vaunted San Francisco 49ers were in town. The Niners had the ball way down at about their own 25. Steve Young dumped a little screen pass over the middle to the greatest-ever wide receiver, Jerry Rice. Rice broke a few tackles (or at least got a few good blocks—tough angle to tell when it was at the other end of the field) and was set free. He sprinted to our end zone, almost in direct line with me. I recall thinking, *Wow… This is a great moment. Remember this!*

Patriots defenders got to Rice but tackled him as he fell into the end zone. He got the touchdown. That is quite Gump-like that I happened to be right there. I can't disagree with you, Mike.

TROUBLE WITH THE BENCH

I was never much in love with weightlifting, and back in the day, the only access to any weight-related equipment was a small nautilus unit that might be pressed into a side room at our high school, and it was usually closed off for general use. I can't remember any gyms existing anywhere. We got strong by being physically active—nothing formal at all. Into college and after though, gyms started popping up and became increasingly commonplace. At the gym, a measurement of manhood was on display in the form of how much weight a guy could throw up. The manhood test of manhood tests was either the bench press or squats. You could work out all day doing anything else, but if you could not put up at least some minimum weight with either of those two testosterone-proving exercises, then you might as well just go home and cut your losses.

My legs were always a strong point, and I could handle a good amount of weight there. So, true to being hard on myself as I always have been, I struggled to accept that I sucked at benching. To be fair and to be honest, I had some issues that held me back. I have this wonky left elbow which I broke when I was in fifth grade. It just never healed appropriately and is all cockeyed (I did an excellent job of hiding it, and no one could tell until I would really show it off and freak people out). Plus, I never liked working out with anyone else and grappled with the thought of asking a stranger for help, especially when it required me to show off a weakness. Requesting some dude to give me a spot was out of the question. Finally, I am also stubborn and don't give myself any breaks, so if I was planning to do one set of ten repetitions and only knocked out nine; that set didn't even count.

Turn the clock ahead to 1998, five years postcollege, somewhere in my late twenties. Dateline: Gold's Gym, Needham, Massachusetts. There I am on the bench. Of course, I am alone with no spotter. By this age, I was able to do some respectable weight. However, all my gains were limited by that inability to ask for help over the years. This night and as I always had done when subjecting myself to getting up underneath a barbell loaded with plates that would come close to equaling my own body's weight, I smartly and purposefully did not employ the pins, just in case! (Oh, by the way, if I have the weaknesses as mentioned above, then I am blessed—or cursed—with the superpower that allows me to predict/foresee potential danger and to prepare for that.)

The lowest acceptable weight for men in their twenties, thirties, forties, and fifties to "warm up" with is 135 pounds.: the barbell and one 45-pound plate on either side. Minimum! Until you could do that without help ten times and relatively quickly, you're not welcome here. These are the stories my mind, which I thought echoed society's norms quite well, would tell me. Then once that set is done, you add to it. You must do a minimum of three sets, and exponential increases must be happening. Doing negative splits (i.e., take plates off) cannot occur until those minimum three sets were completed. This is precisely where my story happened that wintry night, some twenty-two-plus years ago.

Three sets were done. Onto the fourth. A few plates came off (not to worry, only like a five and ten came off; nothing astronomical). Time for the last set. I planned to do ten reps. The pins were off. Breathing/procrastinating finished. Hands in a comfortable spot—just inside those rings. I lift off. One, two, three, foooooour, fiiiiiiiiiiiiivvvvvve, siiiiiiiiiiiiiiiiiiiiiiix, sevvvvvvvvvvvvvvvvvvvvvven. Stop. Big exhale. Eyes were rolling backward a little. Take it down. Back up! Eighhhhhhhhhhhhhhhhhhhhhht! Breathe. Breathe, breathe. Hold it up there. Two more. Down quick. Up wicked slow. Niiiiiiiiiiiiiiiiiiiiiiiiiiiiiiiiiiiiiiiiine! Elbows locked. One more. Breathe. Breathe. Don't quit now. Rack it. You know you're too tired for one more. Rack it. What are you thinking? Don't rack it. You've done nine! You're 90 percent of the way there. Rack it now, and none of it counts. Do it! Breathe. Breathe again. Pieces of spit fly up near the light on the high ceiling. Anyone see that? Here we go. Down unbelievably fast. Up… Nope. Only up about two inches. Stuck. Still two inches off the chest. Come on! Come on! Adrenaline, are you getting this? Where are you? Come on. Adrenaline? Are you gone, adrenaline? Oh god! Here we go! The bar reverses itself and starts heading down again (I think it might be mathematically impossible for something that had started going upward then changed direction and succumbed to gravitational pull, to go back up again). The bar settled on my chest with maybe 175 pounds resting on my 190-pound exhausted body.

Decision time. Now would have been a great time to swallow my pride and ask for help. The gym was pretty packed that night. People were there. People probably had their eyes on me. Someone probably would have helped as soon as I asked. No way! Not me. I don't ask for help—to a fault. So now it's me versus me. Starting to panic as the breathing is obviously compromised with that bar beginning to crush my chest, I had to act quickly. I chose to relieve that pain and rolled the system off my chest onto my stomach. Holy shit! Ten times worse. Now I really couldn't breathe. (Kids, don't ever allow a ton of weight to rest on your abdominal region.) Now I definitely know why our ribs are where they are. It took just about every last ounce of my diminishing strength to roll that bar back onto my chest. Okay. This was getting out of control now, even by my uncompromising standards. *Here we go. It was time to utilize the pinless dump-for-life method. This will be a first*, I thought.

Being a righty, I naturally pushed up on that side and emptied the bar of its plates to my left. Being a first-time dumper, I was in for a shock in the next frame: that f——in bar came spinning around so fast to my right side, as I had not accounted for the lopsided weight scenario, that all the plates went flying off, and the bar was sticking straight up, six feet in the air. The sudden and loud dropping of iron at any gym is enough to stop people in their tracks, and it certainly gains instant attention. For a few years, I missed the nice clothes I had left in the locker room. I was in my car and on my way home less than ninety seconds after racking those fallen plates. About a month later, I finally returned to Gold's and worked hard on my lats!

AIR JORDANS AND MY FIRST MARATHON

The mid-90s were not too glamorous for me—I had a pot to piss in, but it leaked. I was too proud to ask for help. I could not afford to date and went years without going to the dentist or doctor. I chose to eat instead of paying student loans and bounced from crazy job to crazy job. One year, I was a street messenger in Manhattan for Cycling Carriers, and I couldn't afford a bike, so I ran ten to thirteen miles each day, delivering God-only-knows-what to God only knows who. But the epitome of it all probably came in the fall of 1994. My buddy Mike and I were freshly moved into a converted apartment in a third-floor old Victorian home in Jersey City (which had a great view of the World Trade Center if you stuck your head out the kitchen window and craned your neck to the right). Then I decided to participate in that year's New York City Marathon. Might as well, I figured. For the first time in ninety years, there was no World Series to watch, so why not do something else?

I had never run in any race, ever, in my life. I didn't even run track or cross-country in high school (poor grades and Catholic school rules)! But for some reason, I thought I could run this. I ran up and down Montgomery Street, from St. Peter's College to Paulus Hook, several times each way after work, in the dark. Had my Walkman tuned into Z100 or 95.5 PLJ or sometimes broke out the Guns N' Roses cassette when I needed an extra lift. Did that for about a month. I was ready to go! I knew the race hit up all five boroughs, but I didn't yet really know how to get to Staten Island (who does?). Naive, I took the train as far into Brooklyn as I could get to reach that side of the Verrazano-Narrows Bridge, where it all begins—except that it starts on the other side. I figured if I got there early enough, I would just walk across, meander to the starting line, and begin when everyone else starts. Of course, I had no number. Why the hell would I pay to run 26.2 miles? They should pay me.

So don't you know, there are the cops—blocking the Brooklyn side of the bridge. No one can enter. The upper level appeared empty. Not a soul up there. But I was not alone, and the world was way more liberal at that time (more than I had ever realized, and you could do a lot more then in cases like this). Another police officer cordoned off a group of about fifty of us down an on-ramp/side street to the bridge's outlet (a quick check on Google Maps makes me think Dahlgren Place is about right). There I am—Air Jordan high-tops tied tightly, my Red Sox hat on backward (I've always loved pissing off my beloved New Yorkers, and this day I would take any adrenaline boost I could get, so I went for it). I had my sister's 1992 Barcelona Summer Olympics sweatshirt on and a backpack with me (for this sweatshirt and the pair of sweatpants I had worn). It was a chilly November day. I knew I could not last by wearing that many layers once the race got going, but I was too broke to replace anything).

Finally, after our long wait, with helicopters buzzing overhead and a different hum from the small crowd in Brooklyn, it was evident that the race had begun. If it was indeed Dahlgren Place where we were stationed, we were at the two-mile mark of the race! Once the world's greatest runners—in marathons and in many running events, they're referred to as "the elites"—crossed the bridge, the friendly police officer moved the blue NYPD barricade to the side and nodded for our pack. "Have fun and go run," he said.

Ah! I am a marathoner, I thought. Back then, the only people I knew who had ever run marathons were two of my friends' fathers and one substitute science teacher I had in eighth grade. I am kind of making history among my peers. I'm a pioneer of sorts. A mold breaker, if you will. This was quite the big deal. Look at me—running the New York City Marathon. Thoughts of old *Sports Illustrated* articles of Alberto Salazar and Joan Benoit-Samuelson went through my mind (I'm not even sure if they ever ran this race, but their images were in my mind nonetheless). I had learned to be inspired by the great Fred LeBow, the father of this race, who I think may have died just about this time. As it would be, moments into my maiden marathon voyage, these elites were none too pleased to find a backpack-wearing, Air Jordan wannabe, slow ass clogging their path to potential riches. I mean, these people had a realistic shot of being just a few hours away from some lucrative payouts! Then there was me. But did I ever give it my all. I could not let my representation of my Red Sox hat down in the middle of Brooklyn with the world's running stage flanking either side of me. I may not have trained in superb locations that often grace the *National Geographic* cover, but one of Jersey City's newest residents was up for the fight. A bigger guy with a German-sounding accent with snarly English epithets and perfection of the f-word asked me what I was up to on his way by. People were blowing me away.

I couldn't keep up, and my feet were on fire. I was pushing it! *Toes!* I thought. *Run on my toes. I'm faster when I run on my toes.* So I ran on my toes. People were starting to aggravate me. These single and double-digit-number bib-wearers were good! They were really something else, actually. (Years later, I would say this was the equivalent of a fan who thinks he was a great "baller" in school trying to stop a rushing power forward, in the paint, of an NBA playoff game—ain't gonna happen!)

Eight miles into this thing dogged tired but refusing to slow my pace, I found the most beautiful blue porta potty. There it was, in a row of about thirty of them. They were unavailable to the "regular people—the crowd." But, in fact, those were reserved for US—the RUNNERS. Less than an hour into this race, you better believe these elites and the pretty good runners, who were becoming more commonplace in my area of operation as time elapsed, were not about to use the bathroom—not now, not ever. So I had the pick of the litter. As I saw it, the onlookers would see me as having to do what anyone might have to do—use the bathroom. Pride would not be injured by that. So I ducked in there, and let me say, for someone who spent a few deployments in Iraq with porta potties being the best means for toileting, this particular porta potty was like no other. It was fine there. I threw the lid down, locked the door, and tried my best to lay down. Barely able to catch my breath, I spent a good fifteen minutes there! It was great. I hid! What the hell was I doing? I saw red, and I saw blue. Stars were everywhere—in my eyes. My lungs were engulfed. *Oh my god!* I thought. *There's only one way to get back home though—keep running.*

You know what? Save for the Central Park ranger who yanked my exhausted body out of the race within earshot of The Supremes' "Stop! In the Name of Love" blaring at the finish line, I did it. I ran twenty-four-plus miles—as much as I was allowed to run. How about that? Sure, my right knee froze into an unbendable stiff limb as I crossed the Willis Avenue Bridge (field-expedient bare-knuckle massage took care of that slight issue). Still, I got to go home to Jersey City that afternoon with a soaked Barcelona Olympic sweatshirt intact and pride running high. This kid, who might have been slighted by his college administration the year before, ate pasta eight nights a week and had to skip work to go shovel because the money was better, accomplished more than what he knew he could do. I had no doubt in my mind. I just did it.

ONE FISH, TWO FISH, HOW 'BOUT NO FISH

How does someone who grows up in Massachusetts and Maine hate eating seafood? Imagine? What a curse, almost! Clambakes? No thanks! "Hey, wanna join us for steamers?" Sorry, I'd rather have a bowl of Frosted Flakes (seriously!). "Oh, Jay, these lobster tails are to die for! Mmm mmm mmm!" Well, I hope when I do die, I ain't gotta eat lobster tails. According to this month's bonappetit.com recipes, Melissa Miranda of Seattle shared her version of her salmon dish sarciadong isda, which received 4.6 of 5 stars per reviews. Maybe that would be something you'd be willing to try? Nope! Sorry, Melissa. Got any cheeseburgers? I know this sounds snotty of me, but I just can't stand the taste or texture (or smell) of fish or anything that comes from below the meniscus of water. In fact, I am really not that snotty at all (IMHO) if you think about it. After all, I did say I would be all set with a lowly bowl of Tony the Tiger's sweet cereal. But I realize that if I did not live in the world's luxury capital, I would be screwed.

The United Nations suggests that 40 percent of the world's population lives within one hundred kilometers (which is a little more than sixty-two miles) of a coast. Google said only about 10 percent of the world's population lives more than ten kilometers away from a freshwater source of any kind. Three years ago, over 150 million metric tons of seafood went to human consumption, zero of which was tallied up by Jay White. I wish this was a cool thing. Like, say, I didn't eat any Snickers bars, or I could say I never got french fries at McDonald's, or yes or no: Did you, in the past Halloween season, have at least one pound of candy corn? "Ahh (polygraph on?), yes?"

You may have known I have had a chance to travel a little bit, and a few of those times, I got to dip my toes in other cultures for a minute. The time I spent overseas the longest, as a civilian, was in Korea—a peninsula nonetheless. There was fish everywhere! The fish markets in Pusan were otherworldly, like nothing I had ever seen before, with boat-to-market distance cut down to mere feet and a few minutes. Moreover, I attended two Samsung Lions (KBO League) baseball games in Taegu, and there were elder women at the tops of several aisles warming dried fish with kerosene heaters. How do you even hawk that? "Get your kerosene-heated dried fish here! Get your dried fish dried even more by a tank of kerosene! Three-fifty!" (That'd be the English translation I like to twist on how that might go). No Fenway Franks in the KBO. No Usinger's Famous Sausage. No Dodger Dogs. Not in Korea. Dehydrated squid though? You got it!

My first week on the job in Korea illustrates my no-under-water-sourced-food issue quite well. After having accepted a position to teach English for a language institute, I was flown to Seoul in November 1996. I would stay for one week of training before relocating to Taegu (we always spelled that city with a *T* then, but lately, it seems to only appear as being spelled with a *D*—Daegu), where I would be for the duration of my time. Upon meeting the "JEL" Institute owner in the capital, he and a translator treated me to a traditional luncheon at a nice spot located on the street below my hotel. Wonderful, right? Well, I enjoyed the classic experience, which included having to remove my shoes at the entrance (always wear clean socks abroad) and sitting down on the floor with my legs crossed. That was cool only because it was so outside the norm for me! The waiters even brought me a fork, and everyone in the vicinity giggled with delight. (I didn't even ask for the utensil, but whatever!) I guess another part of the tradition was not so cool though: I didn't get to choose my meal—that was for the host to do for me. He ordered me the most enormous damn plate of kimbap (Korean sushi rolls) the restaurant had on its menu. Many of you may be drooling at the thought, and I am sure his gesture was only of utmost generosity, but to me, this was agonizing. These rolls even smelled like the ocean—at low tide nonetheless. In fact, they were even rolled in seaweed. Seaweed! If I don't like fish, I definitely don't like seaweed. But following my own cultural traits, I was gracious and accepting of his generosity, so I downed each and every last one of those sushi rolls. (Imagine a vegetarian friend polishing off a ribeye to honor you!)

Turn the clock ahead one week. Now I am in Taegu with my host family (the owner of the local "JEL" Institute there and the one responsible for my employment and housing). After eating a tiny share of the kimchi (look it up) breakfast I was offered at their residence, they finally showed me to my apartment, and I was on my own! By then, it was about noon on a Saturday, and I had no food and had yet to step foot in my new village. Though I knew there were small markets nearby to purchase items, I just hadn't known what was sold or the local process. So before heading out to plunge onto a page of the Lonely Planet, I took a look in the apartment's refrigerator. There was nothing there. It was completely bare. Then I opened the freezer and found a half-eaten Toblerone bar, rewrapped only in its own beige wrapper. I had never had a Toblerone before, but I pulled it out and took a look. Oh my! That thing was so old that the chocolate had turned purely white. *How long has this thing been in here?* I wondered. *Who left it here?* Oh well! That Toblerone bar was delicious! It ranks at the top of all the candy bar experiences I have ever had.

THAT IS NOT JULIA ROBERTS, OR KEVIN BACON

The following story is true, but it happened about twenty years ago, and the word "emoji" had never yet been said, and now, even when I use them, it is entirely appropriate to read this and not press one. The reason being, there really is no suitable emoji response for this story. So feel free to leave it be (if you read it).

The story:

Boston area's rent was on a continuous rise at the turn of the millennium. It was ideal when four of us were on board to rent out the four-bedroom first-floor apartment on Moreland Street in Somerville. Whenever one of us had to depart, for whatever reason, the common practice had us scrambling to find a replacement renter, and we would all be available to "show the place" should a prospective new roommate want to check out the apartment. After all, none of us wanted to pay the remaining difference should we hold a vacant room.

One Sunday afternoon, a girl who was about my age was the arranged candidate. She took the train to Sullivan Square and the bus to the top of Winter Hill, then walked down to old No. 64. When she got there, I introduced myself, showed her around, answered questions—the usual stuff. After fifteen to twenty minutes, we had exhausted everything pertinent about the place, and I walked outside with her to be courteous as she was going to begin her trek back to Forest Hills and Jamaica Plain by doing what she had just done to get here, in reverse. Just then, I was thinking how our place was slightly unassuming, and I had a feeling that she was only marginally impressed at best, until something caught my eye at the top of our old first floor apartment Street. At that time, rumors had been abounding in the area that something was being filmed, and actors like Kevin Bacon, Julia Roberts, Sean Penn, and even Clint Eastwood may be in the area. *What do you know?* I thought, as there was a gaggle of folks milling about for what would otherwise be a pretty quiet weekend day around there. It looked clear boundaries were setting the scene apart from the riffraff of us who might get too close from about a block away. This most certainly must be a film setup in action.

"I bet they're filming up there," I told this woman, who I barely knew but was hoping would assume a quarter of our monthly bill. "Want to go check it out?" I mean, who has a place where the Julia Roberts and the Kevin Bacon just happen to be filming a movie almost literally outside their front door? What a selling point! Forget how close we lived to public transportation. Let's focus on just how close we live to Hollywood and the goings-on of the national entertainment scene. Why wouldn't I pitch this and convince her to go get a closer look at the commotion? So we did.

We walked the half block up the hill and talked like kids about to see someone famous. After all, that is kind of what we were. Who would we see? *Pretty Woman* herself? Six degrees of Kevin Bacon, in the first degree? Too cool! As we got closer though, real life imitated that dream which was just too good to be true: of all the people there, none of them looked familiar (in the way that a famous person, even though you've never seen them in "real life," might look). In fact, the first thing we noticed was that that barricade to keep out riffraff was actually a POLICE LINE DO NOT CROSS yellow tape. This was not a movie. This was an active murder scene. The vehicle in which the gruesome event had taken place was right there.

We were both speechless. I ended up just driving the woman back to her apartment as it was the right thing to do. We never spoke about renting again with an intuitive and mutual understanding of the given apartment-search scenario abruptly intact. In fact, I don't even know if we blinked again until about an hour after I dropped her off.

I OUGHTA KNOW

Typical Boston area traffic had me stuck—practically parked—on 128 near Dedham. It was summer. I was twenty-five at the time and coming home from a landscaping job. I had my window down. It was so slow-going that I was able to daydream safely. I gotta admit I was sitting there singing along to the radio and a song, which at the time I might not have been mature enough to let my buddies (or anyone) know I knew the lyrics to Alanis Morissette's "You Oughta Know." I was hardly even aware of it myself—until I caught eyes with the girl in the car right next to me, and we simultaneously recognized we were singing in harmony.

TWO CAITLINS IN ONE CABIN

It was about 8:30 at night in early April, and I was listening to the Red Sox-Texas Rangers game on my Walkman while stirring another pot of spaghetti. For one week, upon taking a new position as a writer in the Oxford Hills of western Maine, I was given the keys to the cabin, the paper's owner. Generous as that was and as sweet of a deal as could be offered, the spot was straight out of a Stephen King movie: on a moonless night, it was impossible to see your own hand in front of your face when you pulled into the long wooded driveway.

The cabin was more than a cabin, I suppose. It was bigger than any house I ever lived in, but it was vacant, so until I could find a place of my own, I was allowed to use it for that very brief period. When you opened the front door, there was a den, which led to a dining room of sorts, which then took you to the kitchen area in the backside of the home. That is where I was. Because it was the mid-90s and this spot had no cable TV or little to no reception, my only entertainment option was the lone radio with headphones. I was the only person in this otherwise lovely but kinda-spooky spot. That is, until mid-stir and bottom of the sixth when a woman maybe a few years older than me showed up in the damn doorway between the said dining room and kitchen. As I had (Joe Castiglione) reporting what the Sox were up to—in my ears—I did not hear anyone enter the home. No one had told me to expect any visitors. I thought I had locked the front door.

One look at her, and I did what anyone would have done: I yelled and chucked the stirring fork up at the ceiling. The Walkman's headphones got all twisted on my face. "Who the—? What the—? Holy ——!" Then, stranger than scary (and I could now make out that there was a man with her, standing just behind), the woman calmly and dryly as could be offered her hand out to greet me and said, “Hello, I’m Caitlin.”

So taken aback by the entire twenty-second interlude/change of events, I was left with saying to her the same thing she had just said to me as I shook her hand: “Hello, I’m Caitlin.” What do you know? Two Caitlins in one cabin!

WHAT HOUSE FIRE?

I took a writing position for a small western Maine newspaper in 1996. Having come there from living and working in the New York City area, the adjustment was interesting. There was only a handful of us who contributed written stories each week. On weekends, we had a rotation going where one of us was the dedicated person to cover any news that may have happened. With that, we were issued a police scanner and were expected to keep that on 24-7.

Being that it was a weekly format paper, Wednesday was our deadline for story completion. So when most weekends rolled around, I would have the freedom to leave town and go enjoy my time elsewhere. Having to be anchored in the coverage area when my turn to hold the scanner came about, I thought, *Eh, this is a slow small town.* I thought I could get away with doing whatever I wanted to do. *How much could happen here, anyway?* On one of my weekends, I decided to pack the scanner and hike in a neighboring town. The scanner apparently lost its range and ceased giving reports when I was there. I never thought twice about it until arriving in the office on Monday morning.

"Where were you for the house fire?" my supervisor asked me when he walked in. House fire? What house fire? There was a fire? For real? Nothing happens in this town, I believed, and the weekend I am on duty, I miss that! That would have been the most important news story that happened there since I accepted the job. I was left with no good excuse and reported that I had not heard about it (it wasn't on the scanner). In fact, I was a little perplexed and was curious how he knew about it. "It was my neighbor's house." Oh! (Of course it was!)

THE JAPANESE MAPLE OF NEEDHAM

For a very brief period, I worked as a ground person for a tree removal company in the western suburbs of Boston. I had zero interest in climbing the trees and dropping major branches whilst having one or two chainsaws dangling from me. So I received the branches and debris and would make further cuts to complete the removal process. One day though, there was too much work, and a client in Needham needed a small Japanese maple pruned. (I have no idea if it was a Japanese maple. I don't even know what a Japanese maple is for sure, but I know it was a small ornamental-type tree someone in a Needham development might have, and I want you to get the image.)

Pruning seems pretty straightforward, maybe like painting. Sure, it looks easy, but there's a big difference between a professional painter, for example, and Johnny Do-It-Yourself slapping semi-gloss on the four living room walls. The little deadish branches were no-brainers. But then it gets a little trickier. I had not met the home-owner / tree owner before accepting the challenge and was on the job by myself (with a chainsaw). *Zing*. There goes a branch. *Zip*. *Zap*. A couple more. *Wing*! Another branch is gone. This felt good. This was strangely satisfying. I couldn't stop myself. I started becoming addicted to it. *Zing, zing, zing*. More branches. Now all of these branches were beginning to look troublesome, and they had to go! I took care of all of them!

Later, this middle-aged woman showed up, mouth on the floor. "Oh my god! My tree! What have you done?" I stepped back and took a look at the tree.

I thought a similar thought: *Oh my god! Your tree! What did I do?* I spent the next hour cleaning her gutters out. It was the least I could do.

YOU DON'T HAVE THE SNOWBALLS TO BEEP AGAIN!

Early-spring snow had fallen throughout Boston overnight. That following day, 1.3 million of us were sitting at the traffic light on the Gilmore Bridge, headed toward Cambridge from the Bunker Hill Community College side, staring at the goings-on at the Boston Sand and Gravel site. When the light would turn green, there was nowhere to go, and maybe five cars advanced for each generation. At the time of this little occurrence I will tell you about, I was probably the eighty-seventh car back. Let's say it was eighty-seven—Gronk. Well, car number eighty-eight sees the light go green for the twelfth time and with little to no forward progress. So the pair of eights decides he ought to verbalize his pain in the form of honking his horn at me. "Okay, pal! Yeah, let me move up and rear-end eighty-six. Dude, what are you thinking?" Terry Glenn (Eric Lindros?) decided beeping had been a good approach, so he did it again on green light round thirteen, and apparently, me staring at him in my side mirror didn't hold much clout. So I rolled down my window, easily formed a great baseball-sized snowball (late March has perfect snow for that), and back-flicked it at him. *Smack!* The snowball nailed his windshield right where his mug was looking through. Eights never beeped again. We didn't have a problem.

SECTION 7

ARMY

Five years had passed after I had graduated from college with a bachelor's degree in communications. Other than providing a year plus of doing a no pay local cable TV sports talk show—appropriately named "Obstructed View" to honor the style of professional sports venues germane to our New England nook of the sports world at the time and my propensity to enjoy double entendres, and a few gigs covering high school football for daily newspapers, my degree promised me next to nothing except a bill that was beyond my means.

To make ends meet, I took on all sorts of jobs. Essentially, I ended up doing whatever I could do to pay rent and buy groceries. I had this thing where I would not ask for any help, financially or otherwise, from anyone. That meant I had to find my own place to live—and struggle to pay for it—and eat far too much pasta. As the years started to mount, it became evident that my plan was not working. I might never get out from under this student loan, which may not be as ludicrous compared to contemporary student loans, but when you have not budgeted for one extra penny, that bill gets away quickly. It did. I started to fret for my own future. I was not getting younger, and the opportunities were not pouring in for me. A roommate in the Dorchester apartment, a student at our neighboring UMass–Boston, and a lieutenant with a local Army National Guard unit suggested I do and join the Army like he did. I didn't have to go on active duty. I could start out in the reserves and see how it goes.

But I might be able to at least get some relief from this burdensome student loan and create a bit of hope for a possible future. Nothing else seemed to promise as much at a time when it was needed most. So, I joined. I loved what the Army provided in the friendships, the travel, the push to be physically fit, and the overall challenge. But I, like so many at the time, watched our role change dramatically on the morning of Tuesday, September 11, 2001. A reservist sergeant receiving a phone call from a commander on a weekday morning was not the norm. But mine called me that day. He asked me to rally my squad and report how many troops could be prepared to deploy within twenty-four hours. To where? New York? How? Immediately, I called out of work to my day job and life as I knew it was never the same again.

Our company deployed to Iraq at the start of the war in 2003 and again in 2005. I met some of the most remarkable people I would ever want to associate with, and I experienced days that have forever changed me. I will never be the same. I have no idea what my life would look like had the events of those fateful tragedies never happened. There were days when I have felt bad that such horror had to happen to make positive changes in my life. Now, I focus on remembering that I had nothing to do with the terrorism but instead have only tried to make whatever positive contributions I could, since and because it happened.

BED AND NIGHTMARE AND BREAKFAST

Have you ever stayed overnight at a bed-and-breakfast? They can be nice, but they are not for everybody. If you ever stay at a B&B, as they are often referred to, you will find the locations are typically an older home where the hosts (owners) run the business in the home in which they too reside. Whether describing the house or the town's location, the word "quaint" is typically associated in some fashion. The rooms are all pretty close together, as I have seen, and are no different than you may have had while growing up. In the morning though, the arguable highlight of the experience is the delicious breakfast. Breakfast though tends to feel more like a community event as you may need to sit alongside the occupants of rooms 1–5. Prepare to devour your homemade waffles à la mode with bacon but make small talk with the older couple from Galveston, or the tired-looking younger couple away from their kids for the first time since the kid's births, celebrating their fifth anniversary, or the two dudes taking a break from their Pacific Rim hike, stepping in for hot showers and good chow.

During my R&R (rest and relaxation) from Iraq in 2006, I met my wife in Seattle. One of the nights in Washington state, we reserved a B&B in Port Townsend, which is part of the entry to the beautiful Puget Sound and not far from one of our destinations: Olympic National Park.

What an excellent idea, right? Not if you were that guy having a screaming nightmare in room 7 at 4:30 AM. Anyone ever walked down an antique carpeted twisted staircase feeling like they were not much bigger than that Lil' Sweet dude in the Dr. Pepper commercial? As I walked into the dining area, everyone seemed to suddenly be done eating. Oh well, we had the place to ourselves—my preference anyway.

BASIC TRAINING COOKIE

The military has a way of letting you see life from two angles, really quickly and quite often. I made many rich memories, had all sorts of unique experiences, and met fantastic people in my eight years in the Army Reserve. But what amazes me is how events that may seem largely insignificant are burned into my memory.

Arriving at Fort Sill at midnight to begin basic training, most of us did not know what to expect or what the next several months of our lives would be like. Twenty of us stood at parade rest for over an hour. We formed the shape of a squared *U*. No one knew anyone. It was the Thursday before Memorial Day weekend. The air in Central Oklahoma was already thick and hot even at the stroke of midnight. After the initial screaming by the drill sergeants, who ganged up on us and demanded we depart the bus, we seemed to be alone for quite a while. The silence was deafening. Coupled with the angst of just not knowing when we might get some shut-eye at the end of this exhausting day, the feeling was nauseating.

Then there was Montez, from Phoenix (I would later find that out as we had stayed together for individual training after basic and enjoyed each other's company). Montez was a typical young kid, thin but robust and built like a baseball shortstop. He was full of humor and stories, but no one would know that yet on this night. What I remember most about this first night was when Montez emptied out his travel bag onto the low-lying table in the middle of us all. Out came one of those large unwrapped black-and-white cookies—the kind that was once highlighted on a *Seinfeld* episode. A black-and-white cookie! Even those of us who really didn't know what was allowed or what might be classified as contraband knew immediately that that was definitely not on the packing list. A black-and-white cookie! And it wasn't even touched. He hadn't even attempted to open it yet, as evidenced by the pristine nature of the cellophane covering it.

Though our own fear of humiliation allowed the rest of us to maintain composure and not bust out laughing about that event as it occurred. But Montez's reply to the drill sergeants is what makes fellow soldiers and great friends of mine crack up—to the point of spitting out our beer when we gather annually. Before two drill sergeants had split up the beautiful pastry in front of him, Montez had had to think quickly when asked what his plans for the cookie had been. "I'm saving it for later," he told them. I wonder if he's ever had another black-and-white cookie since then.

ROUNDS OVER BAGHDAD

Thinking about what something might be like and then being in the action of doing that thing are not necessarily the same. There are moments in some of our lives when the activity around us is so surreal. It almost feels like we are outside of ourselves during the occurrence. This brief event I am presenting is not funny to me, nor will it be to you. But I think it's important because it helps define who I am, and I know that similar events have happened to thousands of others, and a similar response may be happening to them as well, even several years after the fact.

Five or six of us were hurriedly pulling up wooden stakes of our "GP Small" canvas tent from the lot next to the mosque across from the Presidential Palace in Baghdad. We had just been alerted that the Third Infantry Division troops, to whom we had been attached to provide combat stress services, were no longer going to be able to offer us cover in that area. I really never found out why this was, but that was not for me to know. My job was to make sure we got our shit together, take what we could, and drive my team to a safer spot—wherever the Third Infantry Division guys were going.

Then the surreal happened! I wish I could type here the noise that I heard for the sake of being accurate. Maybe SSSZZZIP. Or WHOOOOOO-WIT. Rounds were coming in our direction, right over us. Rounds! At us! Over us! Right over us! Right at us? But from where? I couldn't see them. I didn't really look. I had heard the sound of a round, but only when it was going away from me. It's a totally different sound when it's coming at or by you. We had nowhere to run. We dropped down. This came as a bit of surprise despite the location and timing. It may have been about 10:00 AM there then and to that point on what had been a relatively quiet morning. When we returned to retrieve our gear, my hands were shaking significantly. This is not how I would have wanted to think I would react should such a situation ever present itself in life. But here I was, in the midst of the surreal. It was how I was physically reacting. Next is the moment that has defined me: I had to stop shaking. This was not effective, and survival suddenly required effectiveness. I took about two to three seconds, put my hands on my knees, caught myself, and said, "Don't be scared. If I get hit, please just make it quick. You'll probably never even know it happened. Now do what you gotta do!" That was it! I stopped shaking immediately. I removed myself from the fear and rose above the fray.

However, I didn't realize then that my exchange agreement would last the rest of my life. What's worse sometimes is not only do I too often lack having any feelings, but I also recognize this as an issue. (I wonder if it would be better to not even know this was happening.) It's as if I am afraid to be sensitive anymore. I want to be. But I don't know how to go back. I am stuck in this emotionally numb existence. I can help others, which may seem bizarre, but I don't know how to help myself—not when it comes to having feelings. Death does little to scare me (for myself, that is). Getting caught up in little things in life does not faze me. Something that most people focus on—the pandemic, the election, and even the weather—I just don't give a shit about. That stuff all seems so small now! I see why it may not seem small to many people, but once I shook hands with letting go, that was it! I just didn't realize that that was it—forever!

This is all a process. We are all on a journey, and this is mine. I share this so that maybe I can touch someone or someone's family or loved ones going through something like this. I don't know any more about it than anyone else does. But this is who I am—who I have become. I know love. I know forgiveness. I know what I think is essential. I just struggle to feel, or, better said, to allow myself to feel.

Interestingly, I can feel empathy for others, but I struggle to feel for myself. I have found peace and some joy in writing lately. I am grateful for that. It is what I can give right now. I have lots of stories I have not widely shared. I have also done so much work with so many courageous men and women who have seen all sorts of combat, and they, collectively, have provided me with the strength to teach others that it is okay to be scared. It is okay to love. It is not uncommon to also feel numb and detached. Maybe this will not last forever. I don't know. Perhaps someone can share with me how they got by. I would appreciate that.

JUST A COUPLE OF RED SOX FANS

During our pre-mobilization for our second deployment to Iraq, many of us in my Army Reserve unit were coming up on our contract expiration. To provide entertainment while passing the time, a group of buddies and I would urge each other to do different dares from time to time. We knew we would be located at various locations throughout the upcoming year. So to stay in cohesion, we made a plan: we had the whole deployment to see who would acquire a handshake with the highest-ranking person. To win, you had to come home with a photo of yourself giving an over-the-top handshake—the kind where your fingers wrap around each other's thumbs (instead of around each other's pinky).

In-country, I was with a small group running a Combat Stress Control clinic. We invited willing soldiers to take a photo while wearing a Red Sox cap during our year there. Then we would print the image, cut out the faces, and tape up a Red Sox Nation wall/collage. This grew a life of its own and was an excellent morale booster. Then with little time remaining in the theater, I learned that the commanding general of the multinational forces there was a Sox fan and was located nearby. If I could get his ear and just invite him over, our team could add an impressive piece to our wall, and, of course, I would be in a solid position to win the dare competition. I looked him up in the email roster. He was there. I wrote him a brief letter, imagining his visit to us would be suitable for many reasons—for which I would attempt to sell him on—and hovered my index finger over the enter (send) button on the keyboard.

Doubts rushed in, of course. "What if this angers the general? What if I get in trouble? What if? What if?" I was worried. Then I figured, *Well, I am out in three months, so how much punishment could*

I get anyway? Plus, what punishment would be worse than going to Iraq? I'm already here. And one errant mortar, and I will not know how to spell email anyway, so why not? Here goes. I pressed enter. My blood immediately went cold. It was like the first time I would call a girl I liked. After days/weeks/months of contemplating and battling my fear of rejection, I finally pressed that final digit in her phone number—left only to a few terrifying rings and her inevitably answering. Then me having to take responsibility and moving forward. Oh, and by the way, who the hell does an E-6 think he is contacting a four-star general? I was only a few years removed from a few harrowing moments in our first Iraq deployment, and so many things—like this email, for example—seemed frivolous(ish) by late 2006.

I had been a bit reluctant to check my emails the following day (though we had decent internet access the second go-round, we were limited to just two computers between all of us), but I did have a reply from him. *Oh god. What is this going to say? What could he have written back?* I thought. Well, to my relief, the general was a good sport. He acknowledged that he was indeed a Boston fan. The general would be happy to make a visit—and did. A few weeks after I asked him, he showed up at our clinic, wearing a Red Sox cap, and he even agreed to my handshake photo. He congratulated me for winning my dare, and I could tell by the way he addressed me that he must have admired my guts to directly reach out to him. Cooler still, in the photo, I believe I am only wearing a brown T-shirt. Yep.

IT'S STILL ROCK AND ROLL TO ME

I went to army basic training at Fort Sill in Oklahoma. Fort Sill is a military destination for all-things artillery—the "King of Battle," as we included so many times in our cadence during marches there. In the artillery world, what would be called a platoon in other army locations is referred to as a battery. So when we processed through our nine to ten weeks of basic, each of us was assigned to a particular battery. Four batteries made up one company, and the companies were on different training schedules (interacting with another company would not happen). Within each battery, there are four squads, and so on. Our battery had nearly fifty men training to become soldiers in the hot summer of 1999.

Each battery stuck to itself for sleeping, eating, doing physical training (PT), and anything that occurred in our quarters (or "bay"). The company would come together for many road marches, field exercises, PT tests, and anything that took us outside our collective drill area. To make it easier, perhaps, or to drum up camaraderie, each battery was given a name and had a theme. My battery was called the Hell Hounds. I didn't pick the name; none of us did. It was predetermined, and you just went with it.

Further, each individual was assigned a number, which would be used when filing for the arms room. Each time the Hell Hounds—and the other three batteries made up our company—gathered on the drill pad and it was a day to go to the range or check out some sort of sensitive item, we would begin our movement with a chant. The chant would always be the same, and it would start with a number, then the battery's name and theme. For example, let's say Private Snuffy was the lowest number for our battery and he was number 150 (the Hell Hounds had the highest numbers as the other three batteries' numbers were assigned before ours, from the beginning). We would all chant out, "One five zero, Hell Hounds rock and roll!" At that point, Snuffy would appropriately exit the formation and run to the nearby arms room and wait his turn to receive the item(s) of the day.

We had to participate in this ritual, and not being as vocal as possible might get you the attention you may not like. Though I have grown up as a mouther of music in church as a kid, without really being heard at all, a harmonic contribution was not my forte. And I don't care to get too rah-rah either, for whatever reason. I mean I do, but not when I am told to and not when it is all materialized like basic training! That's just me. But for these events, I did it. It was easier to do it than not to do it. We did this exercise many, many times. However, it was not until the absolute final time we did it: to return weapons one day when I heard something different. That WHOLE time, I had been chanting this incorrectly! Oh my! No one noticed? No one said anything! Was I the only one? It goes: "Number, number, number, Hell Hounds lock and load!" Lock and load? Not "rock and roll?" No shit? For real?

NOT "PORTABLE"!

O-dark-thirty, as they say in the military, means some magical time to be up and doing something physically demanding while you and the rest of the world probably ought to be in bed, sleeping. There we were. Fort Sill. O-dark-thirty in the massive and empty parking lot to do daily PT (physical training). We had our olive drab sleeping pads out, our flashlights with the red filter on, and we were dressed in issued gray T-shirts and shorts with a reflective belt across our chests. Push-ups. Sit-ups. Elevated push-ups. Run. Mountain climbers. A ton of other exercises I can't recall the names of—we did it all until we were drenched. At first, this was novel to me. After a while, my crankiness crept in with the compilation of days without much sleep. That's when I noticed the nearby water buffalo, which is the basic army version of a wheeled trailer that transports water to field exercises, parked in the corner of our area. On it read "POTABLE WATER." Being grumpy, I thought, *What a bunch of dumbasses. Can't even spell that right!*

(A month or so later, at our bivouac exercise, I silently said "oooooooooh!" to myself. "My bad!")

MIDDLE EASTERN PENGUIN

Whenever a new doctor would join our team in Iraq, a couple of us would meet them at the Baghdad Airport, pick them up, and take them to their living trailer. On the ride from the airport to the camp, I would be sure to interject a couple of jokes—to test their mettle.

I had two go-tos: I would always tell them that we swim in the canals for exercise. I would wait on revealing that one until we passed a channel. "Oh, yeah, once you get used to the grossness, you can swim in those things for miles!" I never failed to see eyebrows raised or faces cringing, with that look of "what the hell am I thinking for being here?" Then I would tell them, "It's the weirdest thing here. They got these Middle Eastern penguins. Who would have thought, right? The Middle East—so hot. Penguins, we associate with cold. But yeah, they got penguins here. Wait till it's light out tomorrow. You'll definitely see one. They're everywhere." This would arouse wonder and/or an expected "get-out-of-here" type of comment.

With its stark white chest against its black body, the Mesopotamian crow was a unique sight for anyone not local to that area. But once they discovered that that was the penguin I had referenced, it never failed to bring on some combination of laughter or attitude adjustment.

WTF, KID? DON'T EVER DO THAT AGAIN!

I understood that when you are the vehicle driver in a convoy, you do not stop (unless the convoy stops). It could be dangerous to the rest of the personnel if you do. So, God forbid, if a person gets in your way, you need to keep going. When we were slowed down because of a terrain and location, a younger boy, maybe twelve or thirteen years old, jumped in front of my Humvee. He appeared to be just joking around in front of his friends. He did not feel like any more of a threat with immediate observation than what he was doing. I slammed on the brakes! I did not hit him. I yelled at him and warned him with my best international body language to cut the shit because he had no idea how risky that move was—no idea!

In retrospect, many would suggest that I made the wrong move. That boy might be the one responsible for killing or injuring fellow troops after that. Of course, I have no way of telling. I just reacted out of humanity. I couldn't run him over. Not a kid! I just couldn't do it.

SECTION 8

SPECIAL

I can be very random. I am sure that ultra-randomness may not be a trait that gets me too far in a job interview, but I am who I am. I have learned to embrace and appreciate this. Being random is no different from being that baseball pitcher with four or five pitches that he can command, and the batter has no idea which one is next. I like to talk about traveling to a unique destination and discussing our experience with people there. Then I can shift the conversation to some satirical joke about what it might be like waiting in line to visit St. Peter at the Pearly Gates. That is followed by reminiscing about one of Tom Brady's illustrious drives in a Super Bowl win and how best to make venison jerky. I tell my friends how frustrated I am by something or how proud I am of something else. I am a storyteller. I hope you enjoy the stories. I appreciate the mosaic of thoughts they provoke. Who said a particular order was necessary?

MY FAVORITE MOMENT AT YANKEE STADIUM

Going to Yankee Stadium over the years—to see the Red Sox—was never a bowl of cherries. Of course, I knew that going in, and I knew I would automatically bring attention to myself by wearing something Boston: a cap, a T-shirt, my 1976 gray Boston Carlton Fisk jersey. I thought that if I was going to go to the houses Ruth then Jeter Built, I would prefer to announce myself. Should the Sox win, the taste of victory was sweetest when I stayed loyal, I thought. Or if they go down, I wanted Yankees fans to know we Boston fans are solid, and a loss is not the end of us! Regardless, walking down the interior ramps and/or then taking public transportation afterward would often be the moneymaking time to prove whose team, city, and region you support.

Before the Sox broke the eighty-six-year-old curse in 2004, the stale but painful chant of "1918" (those of you who had gone there know what that dreadful chorus sounds like: "Nine…teen … Eight …teen;" it even gives me shivers writing it, still) would undoubtedly ring throughout the hallowed grounds of Munson and Reggie, and Mantle and Maris, of Yogi and Joe D, Lou Gehrig and Don Mattingly, and then Posada and Rivera and Pettitte and as soon as the Yankees took the lead or whenever the Red Sox looked like they were starting to cave, which seemed to happen in every game I had gone to. It was as if the Yankees fans had willed that Bombers team to victory, or willed the Sox to melt. Whatever it was, it worked for them. There was also always that one dude in the upper deck who would hang the 1918 sign over the railing high above home plate—adding a visual reminder to their painful war cry. Being there, watching things unfold in person in any random given game, you started to believe that the curse was more than something *Boston Globe* writer Dan Shaughnessy might have thought was his own creation.

No surprise, but I think the Yankees won the first five or six times I went to see the two rivals square up in the Bronx. I really was starting to feel like Charlie Brown when Lucy pulls the football away from him. I just wanted to walk out of that place the victor, but it was so elusive. One time, it was looking possible for me to witness Boston winning in New York. Mo Vaughn and Tim Naehring hit back-to-back homers—on a day Mo went deep twice—only to see the pinstripers come back by hitting back-to-back-to-back home runs later in the game. New York always outdid Boston, in my presence, and the epithets I received put hair on my chest!

After '04, when the Yankees kowtowed to the Sox in the ALCS and in the way they did it, the mood was different on 161st Street. The night I got to see things come full circle was on an early spring evening on a Friday night in the right field upper deck (definitely not a Boston-friendly area) in 2011. A group of buddies and I ventured in to see the Sox that night, and the Olde Towne Team won. But the win was the second favorite to my sudden ability to quieten otherwise cocky Yankees fans that night. How did I do it? Well, luckily for me, I keep my enemies close. By that, I mean I was probably as knowledgeable about the Yankees team that year as any of their best fans might be. And I certainly have a decent grasp on their history. The Yankees were trailing, right up to the end of the ninth. Many of these arguably spoiled fans (after all, their team has gathered more championships than any other professional sports team) sat there sulking and quiet and unsupportive to their team. I gave it to them! I was standing, hoping to God Papelbon would finish off the night when I called out the once-loud and obnoxious we-can't-handle-losing fans that remained. "This is Jorge Posada," I yelled. "He won you what…, four or five World Series? Are you just gonna sit here and not stand up and root him on? Really? And Jeter… All that he has given to you guys… And you're gonna go quiet on him? How would you like it if that is how he played for you? Huh?" I was loud.

"Stand up, Yankee fans! You got it good! Your team busts their (you-know-whats) for you! Root for them. We want a good battle here. Don't just sit there! Let's go!" I was sober. No one knew what to do with me. I kept going. It felt cathartic. The whole section was a hush except for me in my Fisk jersey! Even though the Yankees had started making the game closer and I started to worry a little, it didn't matter by that point. I tied off the proverbial loop that had been that ancient curse. The final nail in the curse's coffin is the night a Boston fan can walk into the upper deck of Yankee Stadium, wear a hated rival's uniform jersey, and take a boatload of rudeness only to turn around and stuff it back. I shut up a whole section—on a Friday night nonetheless and without chemical assistance. Good night, Bambino. I love ya, buddy!

WHEN THE LADY FELL AT DEVIL'S DOORWAY

It was a Sunday. It was mid-March, and the early-spring warmth was in full force on the eighteenth. Noticing a bevy of Cubs World Championship gear and a smattering of T-shirts and hats representing their lesser-than football team, it seemed the trail was rich with Chicagoans. They had made their way up to what is arguably south central Wisconsin's favorite hiking spot—the East Bluff at Devil's Lake. One of the hikers, a twenty-five-year-old athletic-looking woman, was there alone. She had driven from the Milwaukee area by herself that morning and had wanted to take advantage of the fantastic weather and spend her day outside.

At a pinnacle point on the Bluff, the woman excused herself past a dad and his three children as they all gently descended the narrow rocky path to the trail's iconic masterpiece: Devil's Doorway. The young woman hurried by the family and then bounded up into the rock formation. She took a drink of water from the bottle she had stowed in her backpack and then, of course, snapped some photos that she probably shared with friends on Snapchat or Instagram or on Facebook. Of course, next, she backed up, extended her dominant arm, and smiled to the phone, obviously grabbing images of herself with the picturesque backdrop.

Meanwhile, the family rested on a nearby ledge, next to a couple who were also sitting and admiring the vantage point that is well-used by thrill-seekers who master the park's stealthy stone face for rock climbing adventures. As beautiful as it is here at the Doorway base, this is no place to take things lightly or to do anything reckless; but instead, it is a place to admire and proceed with caution.

The dad was hypervigilant that day. He had to redirect each child when they had acted carelessly on the approach to this peak point. Looking up at the woman, the father, who was sitting and taking in the sunshine, from fifty feet away, noticed something seemed off. Hastily, the young woman packed up her water and her phone, tossed the backpack over both shoulders, and prepared to hop down. It's about five or six feet down from the Doorway to a lower rock plateau. She made the hop, but she had not compensated for the offsetting weight the backpack provided upon landing. Unfortunately, the woman lost her balance and fell backward. The plateau's surface area is probably only about eight to ten feet in diameter. This plateau was not large enough to capture her misstep.

Down below and off to the side apiece, the family of four watched everything unfold as if time had slowed down and the surreal took over. The woman, who had a maroon Cabela's baseball cap on, hit her head on the edge of the plateau and continued to fall. She dropped about fifteen to twenty feet, landing in a supine position, on a ledge that might have been twelve feet wide, above one final wall that ends at the lake below, some sixty to eighty feet straight down from there. The backpack that threw her off saved her life ultimately. Immediately, she began an obnoxious-sounding snore that was both loud and constant. The woman was out cold. At this time, the dad noticed that she was indeed alone. There was no one here to assist her. He looked at his kids and relayed that this was serious, in tone and eye language, and ordered them to stay put no matter what.

The terrain was considerably loose, and the area was better suited for those wearing harnesses and helmets. A young woman, only a decade or so older than his own daughters, was right there, unconscious and in serious need of assistance or else, quite frankly, she might not make it. This was a serious fall! *Obviously, this is a 911 situation,* the dad thought. *But how in the world is help going to get up here, let alone get up here quickly enough?* The dad knew right away that if this had been one of his daughters—or his son—and he was not with them, he would hope there was someone around who would help them if ever that was necessary. So, of course, he carefully and quickly made his way down, making sure not to add to the chaos of the scenario.

Another woman, a mom who was there with her two young sons, also joined the father, caring for the fallen woman. The mom called the police. The dad, recognizing that the young woman, now on her back and only snoring, was not doing well at all. Her eyes were completely white as the pupils had rolled all the way up and back. There was very little blood though—only a little from the back of her head, from under her Cabela's baseball cap—but seemed to contain itself. There was no visual, verbal, or auditory activity happening with the woman who had just tumbled nearly two stories. The dad wondered if her life was fading. He just started talking to her, trying to stimulate her into answering questions.

"What is your name?" he asked, assuming there would be no answer but also unsure what else to ask at first and to hope the simplicity of the question might be enough to miraculously spark her back to cognition. There was nothing. "Are you here by yourself?" he tried. Still nothing there. More snoring. Eyes still rolled back. Breathing slowed. The snoring began to dissipate. With a glance up to his children, the dad appreciated that the three youngsters were aware of the severity of the situation, though he could detect grave fear in their looks. His options were nil now. This situation went from bad to worse, it seemed.

Three years later, the dad struggled to remember what other things he asked her or how he approached the situation in specificity. But knowing help was en route, though her consciousness was not, he stayed there at the site and did not stop. The dad knew he had to maintain any sort of stimulating conversation (albeit one-way). It seemed that without that, she would be gone for sure. It seemed as if her life was truthfully in the balance and had a fifty-fifty chance of going either way, with only the stimulation of talking now (and youth and her excellent level of physical fitness) as the surviving factor(s). At the moment, the dad replayed the entirety of the precursory action in his mind whilst continuing to interrogate her. It was sickening to think: here is this woman who is only twenty-five or so and happily enjoying the weather and the location and may now be in her final moments. How is life so vibrant one moment and gone the next?

Slowly, the young woman regained consciousness. She did not seem to know where she was or what happened at first when she was able to speak again. Those helping made sure she remained lying down as it was difficult to imagine what sort of damage her ribs, shoulders, and hips had sustained. Help arrived. Men appeared on four-wheelers and were dressed for any condition and as if they may need to repel. They wore helmets and carabiners and carried plenty of rope. The men quickly thanked the dad and the mom and politely asked for space. The dad, weak with the feeling that his own blood had drained out of him during the ordeal, climbed back up and thanked the couple nearby who had stayed to help watch his children for him. When the four of them finally left, the mood was somber. Looking back, they saw the young woman remained on her back, with the men caring for her. There was no more recklessness on behalf of the children on the trail back down. The young woman had taught the dad's children a few important lessons: good decisions, respecting nature, and safety in numbers are musts when hiking. In the days, weeks, and months that followed, the dad scoured the news and found nothing to mention the event. He bit his lip and even checked for her name in an obituary. Thank God he saw nothing! Still!

TOUCHDOWN JESUS!

This morning, I took my daughters out. We stopped at Cargo Coffee on East Wash and sat down to enjoy a few delicious treats. The three of us were quietly enjoying what we had ordered when Emma broke the silence. "Touch…down, Jesus," she muttered aloud.

"What?" I said, smiling to myself (and maybe even outwardly). I looked over to a guy in line and saw he was wearing a Notre Dame T-shirt. "Oh," I said, having figured it out.

Sometimes when you are on a highway with your kids, and you know something famous, or somehow worthwhile, might only be a handful of miles off the next exit, get off and go see that place. Obviously, I did this with them at South Bend—three years ago. I just didn't really know how much they had been paying attention. So cool! My daughter knows about Touchdown Jesus. Love it!

THE DENTIST AT THE DENTIST

Fortunately, I am not one of those who require special fear-reduction efforts when I visit the dentist. That said, there was a time about a dozen or so years ago when I needed to remedy a receding gumline with mouth Tommy John-type surgery. In that, tissue required to be transported from the palate to the bottom gum (cringe at that thought as that is an appropriate response), and the novocaine introduction was quite severe, in my opinion, with several deep injections into some pretty raw and sensitive parts of my oral cavity. Youch! Even for me, this was no fun!

However, by far, this was the funniest memory I have ever had in the presence of any sort of medical doctor. What? How could that be? Here is what happened:

So the doctor, who had flat-screen televisions located just in front of each chair, put on *The Oprah Winfrey Show* that morning. Oprah welcomed TV icon Carol Burnett to her program. Carol shared favorite video memories, including the one in which Tim Conway plays the role of a student dentist, and Conway's old pal and sidekick, Harvey Korman, is his first-ever patient. In fact, if you YouTube it, the episode is called "The Dentist." As we were waiting for my numbness to really settle in, the two of us watched Conway jab himself with a novocaine needle in his dominant hand, rendering it limp and useless. My real-life dentist and I started to laugh, even though I was in such a locally anesthetized state that I could hardly string two coherent words together. When Conway proceeded to then outdo himself and jab his own right thigh with the said needle, the two of us—him standing and me bibbed and reclined—just about lost it. My dentist started pounding his own leg and even jostled my shoulder because he could hardly contain himself. The episode is a great one, but viewing it in that exact environment brought it to a whole new level. Our laughs reached a peak when Conway's leg gave out, and he crumbled to a knee. I have always wished to know what the patient and hygienist in the next room were thinking.

AAA—GREAT PAPER

I endured days and nights in my education journey writing papers with standard and electric typewriters, then word processors, dot matrix, and anything else I can't think of between the early 1980s and now. I have even shared some memories in a recently written piece on Facebook. Though I discussed the earlier years in ways that make them seem much less desirable in terms of efficiency and focus and whatnot, there was a time, in 2019, when I would have traded modalities one day.

Writing papers to meet a syllabi deadline was never a great experience for me. In those early years, the detractor was a significant lack of interest (or, better yet, a considerable interest in doing things other than reading an assigned book or studying about a given subject). In the forty-eight-year-old-goes-to-school-on-a-GI-Bill-when-he-has-a-full-time-job-and-three-kids years, it was said job and said life that played the role of challenger. So as I was wrapping up my master's with Edgewood College two years ago, I had spent a lot of nights and/or early mornings getting a big project completed. We would turn these "papers" in electronically, and they were always due by 11:59 PM in Blackboard. (There was no actual paper involved.) Mine was due that night, and I was doing some last-minute touch-ups before the sun came up because I had to get going to work.

My cat, Louie, then jumped up on the table where I was. He landed on the laptop's keyboard and, with some genius stroke of his left paw, reduced my work to this: AAA. Yup, three big old capital *A*s. That was it. All gone. Irretrievable. Probably about fifteen pages gone. "Didn't you save your work?" Well, I had, but this was opened to get completed, and for whatever reason, it was not retrievable. "What about that backup/undo button?" Believe me, I was pressing that thing as if my life depended on it. I called my tech friends. Nothing. I even called Edgewood's IT team. Nothing. "Did you call Blackboard?" I even called the folks at Blackboard. No solutions existed. So I went to work, pissed off.

Don't ask me how I pulled it off, but I figured if the Patriots can come back from twenty-five down with seventeen and change minutes to play in a Super Bowl, I can do this. I did it, basically from scratch (and memory). I got the work completed before 11:59 PM. That day, I wished I had been using the Smith Corona.

Hats off to all the other adult learners out there: I know it ain't easy, and you often graduate with little to no fanfare. Congratulations on keeping your nose in the playbook and enduring what you do!

SWAN RIVER

It doesn't matter how tough you think you are; you should never mess with nature. Always respect the ocean, the water you swim in, the rocks you climb on, the vegetation all around you and, most definitely, the rest of the animal kingdom. If you don't show respect, nature will force the issue on you until you do! This will happen every time, with no exceptions! So here goes a little story, of course.

My late buddy, Tommy, a Marine from Newark who was actually born on November 10 and who gave me my kayak and used to take me on the Connecticut and Mattabesset Rivers in Cromwell for pre-sunrise paddles in warm months, would warn me. "You gotta watch out for those beavers when you come onto the Mattabesset (from the Connecticut)," he would say. I heeded his message, though I still maintained a bit of an "okay, Tommy, whatever" attitude. One time, in that exact area, I floated ahead of Tommy, and we got fully onto the Mattabesset and were approaching a second big bend. It was just about dawn, and the light was starting to split the trees when I heard what I thought was a gunshot. "Bejesus, what in the ——," I said aloud as I naturally ducked my head and shoulders down immediately. Tommy started cracking up behind me. He mutter-chuckled "I told you!" with that thick Italian Jersey accent in his Tommy-Marine-Corps way. I never even saw that beaver, but the message was loud and clear! There was no way I was going to interrupt that flat-tailed river rodent, its dam, or even go anywhere in the vicinity of where that water slap emanated. Dear God! Good job, Beav. You win.

I gotta be honest. After that, I kind of wanted to conquer this newfound river fear and take to those waters solo. I did, albeit with one modification. Instead of entering in the Connecticut, I loaded in behind the Dunkin' Donuts, on the other end of the Mattabesset (away from Mr. Beaver). Out there alone and processing through my heebie-jeebies as a new day was cresting, I worked my way into a good workout. I probably traveled two or three miles down the Mattabesset to where it looked like it was narrowing up ahead. I had not been on this part of that river before this, so my eyes were wide, and my sensors were keen. "Oh, wow! Would you look at that," I said, either only in my head or possibly slightly audibly. A beautiful swan was about fifty yards in front of me. Wait, there were two of them. They were majestic. Their color was stark and stunning in the morning glow. I felt fulfilled as if my week was made for having gotten up early and taken the time to be out here this day to see this sight. I couldn't resist, so I got closer. It was two gorgeous white swans and me. They were smooth; they floated in silence. I thought of the iconic Boston Common boat ride, Tchaikovsky, and "The Ugly Duckling" story. Then suddenly, the one in the back morphed into the devil. The two swans had been flanking a baby. Good Lord. The swan closest to me was no longer majestic. That dude was all business. I was clearly at the wrong address and needed to be out of their neighborhood. There was no passing them, and, like it or not, my kayaking adventure for that day had reached its peak. "You got it, swan! All you, man!" I don't think I have ever gone kayaking on a river alone since.

(For those of you who like to Google everything, let me save you a moment. A baby swan is called a cygnet. I know because I just Googled it.)

AND BEHIND THIS CURTAIN

Who really knows what to do the first time their kid is born? Who really knows what to do when their first kids are twins? I certainly did not. So I am at the Middlesex Hospital in Middletown, Connecticut, the night after Jessi had Anna and Emma. Jessi was with Anna, resting in our assigned room. I had gone to be with Emma in the nursery. The head nurse, who is also the lactation consultant there, checks me in, gets Emma, takes me over to a rocking chair, and hands me a bottle to feed the baby. Then, she asks me to grab that trifold-y makeshift curtain-y thing (the one new nursing moms appreciate having for privacy) and erect it around the area of the rocking chair. She proceeds to convince me of the power of skin-to-skin contact for the bonding experience and insists I remove my shirt while I hold Emma. What am I supposed to do? I can't tell her she doesn't know what she is talking about. I can't say no and deprive my sweet Emma of bonding. But I am still Jay White, and walking around the inside of this hospital without a shirt on just feels wrong.

Once I held Emma, I took a seat, began to rock, and started bottle-feeding her in my whole new setup. Then the nurse promptly left the room. *End of shift? Are you kidding me? Whoa! Whoa, whoa! Where are you going, lady? Don't just leave me here like this. I don't think I ever even saw her again. Is this a prank?* I thought. No surprise, in comes the new head nurse, who had no idea I was there because she could not see me, and shortly after that, naturally, an actual mom comes in and requests a little peace and solitude. The surprise on the three of our faces when that mom came to snag my curtain.

MUSEUM OF WICKED MODERN ART

Every February, I traveled with groups of Connecticut veterans to various museums in Boston or New York. We all appreciated "getting out of dodge" in the middle of winter, and we were fortunate to have such rich cultural options relatively nearby. About ten years ago, we went to the Museum of Modern Art in Midtown Manhattan. I had arranged this well in advance, thus providing us with complimentary tickets and a wonderful welcome by the head of visitor services (this included prime space for our extended cab van; otherwise, this would have been a nightmare to park at this location). Nine veterans enjoyed the day and, of course, provided hearty laughs that I cannot forget still. One of the guys tried to touch van Gogh's *Starry Night.* (That was actually not that funny when it happened but gained humor on the ride home when we goofed on that vet for having done that.)

The MoMA, as it is often referred to is pretty cool—lots of contemporary (hence, "modern") pieces which may be familiar to many: Andy Warhol's *Campbell's Soup* collection (I had thought all of those cans were painted on one canvas until I was dwarfed by the display in person), Dali's melting clocks piece, one of Eddie Munch's versions of *The Scream* was there when we went. Some of Keith Haring's work, to name a few. There were galleries dedicated to photos and galleries containing tapestries and galleries with rare collections and, even more, galleries housing other unique pieces. It was clear that many of this winter weekday morning's visitors were likely MoMA members. These folks walked around businesslike. There was no one referencing brochures or the maps hung near the staircases and elevators. They were moving around purposefully, often with a sketchbook with various artistic pencils at the ready.

It was quiet, of course, and each piece, even the broken-TV display that played a loop of Dan Rather doing the nightly news in black-and-white, had a small plaque that named and dated the art and credited its maker and the maker's location. For example, the said television set's placard would have read something like "News at Night, 1976. Joseph B. O'Doughnuts, United States." The regulars, if you will, worked at recording this information in their journals or in their memories or both. Nearing the end of our excursion here, one of our buddies, Jake, decided to charge his cell phone in a nondescript outlet at the bottom of a wall in the let's call it the "Dan Rather TV Gallery." When he did, his wire inadvertently draped below, forming a neat figure eight.

This poor woman, who was clearly not participating in her first rodeo here, was beyond perplexed when she stumbled upon the attractive yet never-seen-there-before creation. In fact, her discomfort, albeit silent, was prominent enough that most of us took notice. For the life of her, she could not figure out who might have constructed this oh-so-familiar-but-how-delicately-intricate original. Pure genius! Life imitating art. Art imitating life. So refreshing. How eclectic. *But whose work is this?* you could nearly hear her thinking. *What is this called? That wire! That figure eight! All so lovely! Well done!* The bewilderment on her face when Jake excused himself for passing her and unplugged his phone was worth the price of a membership.

(Note: For those who love art, I do not mean to make you cringe and will give due credit. Of course, Dali's work is not called Melting Clocks. That is the *The Persistence of Memory*, which I did have to look up. Also, it is Edvard Munch who did *The Scream*, not "Eddie." But my art is my writing, and I thought "Eddie" added humor, plus if I had written "Edvard," it would have looked like I was doing too much research and not enough relying on memory. Truth be told, I did remember it was called *The Scream*, but I could not recall that artist's name. Warhol? I did not have to look that one up.)

"ED, FROM BROCKTON"

The start of the 2004 Patriots season was quickly approaching, and fans all over New England were getting pretty stoked. Tickets to the opening night game versus Indianapolis were very hard to find. In fact, if you didn't own or know someone who held season tickets, you weren't going—unless you could figure out a miraculous way to win tickets, of course. That's where this story happened.

WEEI in Boston was the main sports radio station then, and it seemed that so many people were tuning in so often. My buddy Aaron and I were driving around Boston one afternoon when we concocted a clever idea. Aaron's dad, Ed, is a huge Pats fan and was known to keep his ear close to the goings-on of the team. In fact, Ed had prided himself on the few times he had previously called into "EEI" and considered his calls "good ones"—as in he was "one of the smaht callahs" who had made good points during his airtime. In other words, Ed was an easy target for some prime-time pranking.

Knowing Ed was familiar with the names of the primary talk show hosts and even the jockeys who did the sports flash updates every twnty minutes, we chose a somewhat familiar—albeit kinda obscure—name to reach out to Ed. I played the radio personality. I called Ed to alert him that because his name and phone number had been on record from his previous call-ins that year, he was eligible and selected to be the lucky contestant for that afternoon's trivia question. And the contest bore a pretty sweet prize: a pair of tickets to opening night, Patriots versus Indianapolis, at Gillette. (He had been informed that all he had to do was answer one question correctly. His boat was in the slip, and all he needed to do was tie it up, if you will.)

We knew this was borderline savage, but the humor would last a lifetime, and the opportunity to do it was smaller than a closing crawl-space window. So we did it. We called Ed, and I ("Wallach") got him on the phone. I told him about his great fortune and that he just needed to dot the Is and cross the Ts, and two prime spots would be reserved for him and a guest. It was apparent in his response that he was dumbstruck. But as incredible as this seemed, Ed also understood that it was possible to have won after all. He had called in and probably provided identifying information. Plus, if you have never won or been in a position to win something like this, you definitely don't know how the "behind-the-scenes" logistics roll. So we had him—right where we wanted him.

Ed was told to stand by and wait for the question/contest if he was willing and interested in participating. Of course, he was, and of course, he did. (Later, we were told by Aaron's mom, Ed's wife, that Ed had even locked himself in one of their home's quieter rooms to enable a better chance for him to focus when his big moment was to come following this "standby.") In my car, we had the live (real) WEEI broadcast on the radio and blared it in the background to make it all seem as realistic as possible. I played down my own excitement, using a tone as matter-of-factly as possible. We got Ed back on the phone, and adding a little extra sauce to the flavor of the moment, we put him on hold again (we rested the flip phone against the dashboard/radio speaker to increase the "realness" of the contest). We then turned down the car radio's volume and waited a few long silent seconds. I (still "Wallach") addressed Ed as if I was recording our interaction for a wider listening audience, using on-air later that day (in case he were to answer correctly and win). So that sounded something like this: "Hello, 'Ed from Brockton!' You have been chosen as WEEI's lucky contestant to win a pair of those coveted Patriots tickets to opening night to see banner number two being raised on Thursday night in Foxboro at Gillette Stadium. Are you ready, Ed?" Ed, clearly nervously excited, was like: "Oh yeah!" with a ribbon of "let's-just-get-to-the-contest-so-I-can-win-those-tickets" attitude.

"Okay, Ed, here we go! Ed, for a pair of New England Patriots-Indianapolis Colts tickets this Thursday night, please tell me, What number does Tom Brady wear?" That question is about as simple as asking Ed what state he lives in.

Ed threw out one of those verbal *tttt* sounds (the sound you make with an escape of air between your tongue and upper front teeth when you cross between feeling relieved and verbally expressing that you know the answer to something). He was almost suggesting that the question was too easy and insulting his football intelligence. Ed belts out, "Twelve!" No response from me/"Wallach." Ed repeats himself, with increased volume and more urgency: "TWELVE! Tom Brady wears number twelve!"

I add to the tension: "Ed? Are you there, Ed? Hello, Ed! Ed?" Naturally, Ed is reacting to all of my pleas to get him "back on the recording."

He starts yelling, "Hey, it's Ed! I'm here. I hear you! It's Ed!" Ed was getting frantic, recognizing that his once-in-a-lifetime opportunity was all but eluding his figurative grasp, as if it might happen in an unpleasant dream. When the call ended, poor Ed was just like most everyone else: ticketless! Thankfully, Ed is good-natured and laughed at his own ability to fall for such tomfoolery! For some reason, I never really felt too badly about this prank until I was writing it now. So mean of us! Goodness! (But I still crack up thinking about it.) Thank you for being a good sport, Ed!

WELCOME HOME, THIRTY-SIX YEARS LATER

My friend Garrick and I were new outreach counselors at the Vet Center when we decided it would be nice to try to merge some of the new Iraq and Afghanistan veterans for the sake of camaraderie and physical fitness. Garrick was in Manchester, New Hampshire, and I was in Hartford, Connecticut. In 2005, we gained permission from the Boston Athletic Association to ruck march the entirety of the Boston Marathon route on the third Monday of April, Patriots Day, the day of the world's grandest marathon. We gathered about a dozen of us in Hopkinton, where the race begins, and stepped off at 4:00 AM. One veteran brought it upon himself to carry a quite sizable American flag.

As we worked our way through the predawn of Ashland and Framingham, the roads were still quiet as only volunteers were beginning to set up water tables and medical tents. I think we were one of the first groups of veterans to do something like this, so we may have thrown a lot of people off when they saw our gaggle stroll by out of the inky darkness.

A group of veterans from the Boston Vet Center joined us in Newton, as planned. Our total count was now up fifteen to twenty. By the time we got to Comm Ave. and could see the Citgo sign, the Red Sox game, which traditionally starts at 11:00 AM that day, was already underway. At this point, we realized the marathon fans were beginning to quickly grow in number as people were ponying for good viewpoints. So we took our group and neatened things up: we made two columns and kept the flag-bearer at the front.

Once people started recognizing that this was a group of recently returned combat veterans, they began to clap and cheer. As we got closer to Boylston Street and the finish line, the crowds and the cheers grew bigger and stronger. It was really quite a moving experience to be part of that, and I think it made those veterans feel pretty special. The spirit was peaking when my highlight of the day (week, month, year?) happened. Tom, the team leader for the Boston Vet Center, a Vietnam veteran and a local gentleman who had grown up in this area and never really got this sort of "welcome home" feeling that we were getting that day, asked for the flag for a moment. With his tall frame and iconic beard, Tom held that flag up high and decided to run a loop around the columns of veterans. The crowd went nuts. The sun was splashing down on us; the warmth of the day was setting in. *Oh my god*, I thought. "*This is the first time Tom has been recognized like this by his hometown people. And he has been back from Vietnam for thirty-six years!* Tom was sprinting by the end of his second loop. It was as if he was nineteen again!

FIRE IN MELROSE

The concrete days were always the most difficult. The mixing truck would show up, as planned and never late, outside the residence of a Melrose home, and the three of us on this small construction crew would line up with our wheelbarrows and start hauling. It seemed the portal entrance for concrete was "out back," and the truck was always pinned in the street—fifty yards away. As anyone who knows the suburban Boston landscape, "out back" could bring on numerous challenges—dips and dives, bushes, trees, slopes, rocks, sogginess, slipperiness, you name it. "Out back" also seemed to lead to one more challenge: never was the concrete's final destination without some significant man-made barrier. Of course! This is New England, where life is kinda hard. And if it's not, we make it hard! After all, if you're not in pain, you ain't working! And if you ain't working, what are you doing? Even my grandfather had a framed quote above the guest bed in his Massachusetts home: "He who rests, rots!" This day, the barrier was a three-and-a-half-foot block wall.

We had to get umpteen yards of fresh, wet, heavier-than-hell concrete into a crawl space, from the truck out front, through the side yard, and up over the two-by-ten plank that formed a ramp. I was fortunate Kris, our foreman and the youngest of the three of us and one of the funniest dudes in Boston, took pride in his raking skills and insisted he would be the one inside, smoothing out what we poured inside. By no means was he skipping town on the heavy load-bearing wheelbarrow hauls. He would do that too. He was just a workhorse and would do both.

A few things about these concrete days: we always managed to schedule the deliveries for a Friday (this allowed time over the weekend to ensure the pour could settle without us jeopardizing it). We also planned to go to a favorite roast beef sandwich shop in. So for all those forearm-burning jaunts from the truck, through the yard, up the plank, and into the proposed crawl space, it was more tolerable knowing that the piled-high protein-rich melt-in-your-mouth thinly-sliced deliciousness on a fresh onion roll was just around the corner. Quite honestly, I think the key ingredient in what makes a meal great and/or what puts a meal over the top is the eater's attitude when devouring it. For us, we went to Billy's Roast Beef, knowing we deserved to be at Billy's Roast Beef. When we went there, it was an entitlement. We didn't go to Billy's on a slower day. No, going to Billy's was a self-reward type of event, and there would be no hemming and hawing about, "Hmm, I'm trying to watch what I eat, maybe I shouldn't." Oh no. We knew we should. By the time we pulled the pickup into the little joint's parking lot, our arms were heavy and sore. Our legs were rubber. We were tired—but a good tired. Bring on the roast beef! Get two!

It was finally spring, and we saw Billy's had set out tables and chairs on the little patio out front. Of course, we opted to sit there. I plunked down into a seat, facing the street with my back to Billy's, and was beginning to unwrap this holy harmony when I noticed smoke rising from what appeared to be the roof of a multistory home about four houses down. We were tired and not exactly in the mood to get up (and stall the commencement of devouring the roast beef sandwich). Kris, Tenzin—the other crew member and a native Tibetan gentleman who now lived around the corner from my apartment in Somerville and with whom I shared rides—and I kept an eye on the smoke. It gave off a concerning sensation though, and we all could detect that. Could this be the start of a more extensive house fire? Oh jeez!

We started eating but kept watching as no one else on the patio seemed to notice the smoke. We did not see people going in or out of that home—about two hundred feet away. The smoke increased in volume and darkness. It was quickly getting to the point where we had no choice but to do the right thing and investigate. What if people were in there—showering or sleeping or doing whatever—but they didn't realize the dangerous situation they might be in? We couldn't just sit there and take it anymore. We wrapped up our barely-eaten sandwiches, chucked them in the truck, crossed Main Street, and headed to the house. Upon getting closer, it was evident that there were two or three dogs inside. They were barking that loud and nervous kind of bark. We did a quick look around the outside. No people. The smoke was definitely up on top, with the dogs inside. I banged heartily on the front door. Nothing! Banged again. Still nothing! Okay, now the dogs are really riled up, but these little guys are in trouble. Is no one home? Maybe they are trapped there. Maybe someone fell down the stairs, they live alone, and they are lying there unconscious. My mind can make up some pretty wild scenarios. I then hurriedly walked around to the side door via the three-season porch. Knocked again. Still nothing! Just scared dogs were losing their minds (but about to lose more than their minds, I was afraid).

I turned to Kris and Tenzin, who were right behind me, and asked, "What do you guys think?" We mutually agreed it seemed pretty evident that a 911 call was in order. So I called. I stated the issue and gave the address. I provided my name. I felt pretty helpless, and I was second-guessing myself that maybe I should have just tried to rescue those dogs myself right then and there. But I thought, given the circumstances, we did the right thing, and hopefully, the fire department can come down here and get them quickly (without me having to break down a door). We immediately heard a siren off in the distance and figured our work here was done. So we turned and began heading toward our work truck to retrieve our sandwiches and resume eating. No sooner did we get another ten paces away when a grumbled old voice in a Boston accent belted out: "WHAT DO YOU WANT?" The three of us stopped in our tracks and looked at each other. Our eyes and mouths shot wide open with the sound of simultaneous short inhale, followed by a nervous and almost inaudible chuckle. We were relieved that those dogs were probably going to be okay. But we were thrust back into childhood, reminded of that grumpy old person yelling at us to "go away" some twenty years prior. We were also aware that this dude's day is about to change here in a minute. We looked back. The older guy was standing on the porch. He didn't care what we had wanted, based on his tone, but seemed more annoyed that we had dipped into his time and privacy. *Oh boy! This isn't going to be good (for him)*, I thought. If he was indeed annoyed by us, what was about to come his way will quickly have him forgetting we ever showed up.

By now, the sound of distant sirens was getting closer and was growing in number. Of course, we knew what that was all about—he didn't. Yikes! "Hi, sir!" I tried to maintain composure despite his attitude. After all, I knew something he didn't, and I would prefer to be gonzo when the apparatus showed up—and that time was diminishing rapidly. "We saw some smoke and heard your dogs barking, so we just wanted to check it out!" I'm doing a slow backward walk at this point (as is Kris and Tenzin), trying to talk to him but also wanting to gain some separation!

"SMOKE?" he repeated me, but with a particular snarl, then, in a very thick New England curmudgeonly drawn-out-for-purposes-only-to-elaborate-his-point type of way, said (note to reader: for appropriateness, make this quote last about ten seconds), "WHAAAAAT? THAT'S THE GODDAMN CHIMNEY ON THE OTHER SIDE OF THE GODDAMN ROOF."

"Oh! Is it? Okay then. Just wanted to make sure," I answered and thought I must sound like Clark Griswold in *Christmas Vacation* when he quickly but sarcastically responds to the lingerie saleswoman when she shares what her name is. I figured that was enough. He wasn't worth conversing with, and we had less than a minute to evade the scene. We actually tried to return to the outdoor patio seating area, but we couldn't take it when truck after truck after truck came barreling toward the house. It was very unsettling. My Catholic side was chewing me up alive. I didn't do anything wrong, but I somehow felt like I had, and I knew the potential amount of Hail Marys needed to absolve something like this was mounting quickly. I don't know if my knees had it in them to stay kneeling at the altar for that long (even though I can whip out a Hail Mary in less time than Bo Jackson can run to first base from home plate). We left. We must have pulled over three or four times on the way back to the work site, allowing even more fire crew to pass, cringing each time. I hope the dogs were okay!

TEN VETS IN A VAN

When Curt Schilling was pitching for the Red Sox, I had contacted him as he was part of a program that some Major League Baseball players were involved with supporting US troops and veterans. Try as he might, he was unable to get me a handful of tickets for a group of veterans interested in attending a game as part of an outing. At that time, Fenway Park was sold out night after night after night. Instead, Curt landed me ten tickets for a game the Red Sox would be playing at (old) Yankee Stadium toward the end of the 2007 season.

It turned out to be a really great event. Curt welcomed us to go down onto the field and remain there for the duration of batting practice. He took a group photo with us and individual pictures with anyone who wanted one. Having come to the Bronx that night from central Connecticut, the roster of veterans was pretty evenly split between baseball loyalty: half pulled for Boston, and the other half were Yankees fans. No matter, it was a great time and an excellent chance to make memories.

After the game though, the van I was driving was shoehorned into a tight parking spot in the Yankee Stadium lot under Major Deegan. Being veterans and always team-thinking, one vet hopped out and agreed to stop the flow of parking lot traffic for me so we could pull out. This vet had a Red Sox jersey on, and the two young men in the advancing souped-up pickup truck did not like that, apparently. They were prepared to hit—or at least scare—our guy. Our volunteer ground guide enforced a move that made the driver of the pickup stop in reaction to this. Further, that driver and his buddy decided it was time to get out and pose potential physicality. Those two men with the New Jersey plates and the pretty truck did not realize that our van was full of ten recently returned Iraq and

Afghanistan veterans. I get goosebumps thinking about how quickly our van unloaded—no one stayed behind—and any differences we had had between our loyalties in sports' biggest rivalry was no longer a factor. Those two young men's mouths hit the floor when they realized what hornets' nest they had just punched. They could not get back in that truck fast enough. Calm prevailed. No one got hurt.

PROOF IS IN THE PUDDING

I'm on the phone with this first-time client. I'm trying to be professional and build some rapport. Never fearful to utilize a cliché, analogy, or proverb to help bolster a point or prove I understand theirs, I chose to pull out the evolved "the proof is in the pudding" on this day. But so does he. We could have said "jinx" because the two of us said that exact same thing at almost the exact same time. I was thrilled. I commented on how great it was that he thought to use the same saying I used, and I pointed out that we said it at just about the same time. I kind of kept carrying on perhaps a little longer than was necessary about our matched use of the phrase and how you don't always hear people use that one anymore. Anyway, as I carried on and moved through the assessment, I recognized that everything I was saying was echoing.

THE COMMUNITY INTERVIEW

I once took part in a community phone interview for a prospective employee. When the call was placed, it was put on speakerphone, but the interviewee never answered, and it went straight to voicemail. Nine of us had notebooks and questions, ready to participate. Our leader left a message. An awkward silence then filled the room. To break that, I made up an impromptu song using the interviewee's last name as the base. Everyone laughed. I did my job and lightened the situation. The body language around the room was that of relief, comedy: "Oh, Jay, you're so funny. Thankfully we have you for that!" That all changed as the next sickening sound entered the room about twenty seconds later: BEEEEEP.

PANTLESS IN DC

One of the most remarkable experiences I had in my career at the VA was when I was chosen to represent the department as a subcommittee member on PTSD. That committee's recommendations went straight to the undersecretary and then, if accepted, on to Congress for potential action that would directly affect our veterans suffering from this harsh condition. The group consisted of about a dozen members of the VA, mostly doctors and published psychologists plus four of us from the Vet Center. I was least tenured and still working on the graduate degree that everyone else had already earned years before. I knew my place on the team: I was at the end of the proverbial bench. I was the Eddie the Eagle of ski jumpers, the Rudy Ruettiger of the Fighting Irish. The Lupus of the Bad News Bears. I was a member nonetheless. It was a fantastic opportunity to be with a group that can really make a difference—with some of the greatest in the field.

The committee would hold monthly phone conferences and then get together once or twice a year at the VA's central office, a block or two behind the White House and Lafayette Square in Washington. Our meetings started early and went throughout the day. We followed a tight schedule, and many important people would stop in and provide brief updates on critical facets for the group to consider for the development of our report. I always enjoyed traveling to these annual or semiannual gatherings. When we lived in Connecticut, I could take the Amtrak Acela the day prior, and I found it pleasant to sit back, relax, and absolutely zip through the Northeast Corridor in under five hours—only nine stops. I would drive to New Haven's Union Station, park, check in, and quickly board the DC-bound train.

One of the times though, I was walking up to the station and crossing Union Avenue when I had less than fifteen minutes to spare before the Acela was due to pull in. (When this thing arrived, it didn't stick around long, providing just enough time to board, find a seat, and put your stuff down. Missing it would require a lengthy wait and would eat up any time you might have to spend touring around the capital city later.) Before I stepped onto the sidewalk closest to the station, I was struck with a harsh reality: I forgot my pants! I didn't pack pants! None! I have no pants! I have toothpaste and floss, but I did not bring pants to wear to the central office! My committee-mates dress very well. They use big words. They're wicked smart. I was wearing "travel jeans," the same ones I had used to cut the lawn that day. Jeans were a no-go. I'd be better off lying and saying I couldn't get there than to show up wearing jeans. Walking into central office wearing jeans would elicit the same feeling that may accompany the guy who meets the family of a big crush only to realize he has dog shit on his shoes when he arrives at the house.

Any plans I had had to check out one of the Smithsonian museums or walk to the Vietnam Memorial again were dashed. My evening's plans suddenly looked much different. I had gotten on the train, made it to DC, and immediately went to the first store offering some semblance of men's clothing. It was Forever 21. Forever 21! Me! At Forever 21! My options were slim. My reputation was on the line. My livelihood was at stake, and the clock was ticking. I was the lowest person on this committee's totem pole, and even if I didn't play a significant role, one thing was for sure: I better at least dress the part.

Forever 21 was right inside the stunning main terminal of Washington's Union Station, immediately beyond the entrance from the hectic platform. When I walked through the clothier's glassy doors, dudes started chirping into their wrist cuffs—communicating with fellow clerks, sending out an all-points alert that they had a suspicious character roaming their wide bamboo aisles. No "hello!" No "can we help you with something, sir?" Nope. Just a bunch of stink-eyed Secret Service-like twenty-one-year-olds eyeing me up and down. I hated being there slightly less than I hated my predicament. There were one size 36 by 34 pants in the whole place. Just one!

Apparently, 36 by 34 is the size of those who aren't twenty-one forever. Without trying them on and within moments, I was the newest owner of a pair of the most unique golden-like khaki pants I had ever seen. I may not be much of a shopper, but $65 seemed like a lot.

I held onto my receipt and hoped to return these blond beauties on my way out of town in two days. I had extra time and was bent on being frugal, and I was determined to return my purchase to the snarky team at "F. Two to the One." Thinking I was pretty slick, I concocted a novel idea: I spent the entire evening walking from Hay-Adams to the Foggy Bottom and all around Patrick Ewing's Georgetown campus. But there was not one Goodwill or other thrift stores to be found. No Salvation Army. No St. Vinny's. There would be no last-minute save for five bucks. Nothing! So I had to eat the expense. These sharp-looking pants were mine, all mine. Worn begrudgingly at first but looking the part, they got me over that hump and saved me from myself. (To close the gap between the number of "times worn" versus "price spent," you shouldn't be surprised to hear that they're still a regular on many a Zoom call more than a decade later. And thank God this didn't happen last year because me wearing skinny jeans—I think I would have quit.)

THE MAN, THE MASCOT

When my twin daughters were three years old and lived in Connecticut, I took them to the New Britain Rock Cats' Double-A minor league game one summer night. As much as I love baseball, I knew how this game would go: we'd maybe watch one full inning from our designated seats, and from then on, you would most likely catch us in the little playground area that was behind the stadium's third base side—entirely out of view of any of the playing surface. (*Oh well!* I thought! I got an inning in, and I was hoping to slowly share my love for our pastime with them. So these small steps were part of a bigger plan.)

Like many minor league venues, the Rock Cats were mascot-heavy, and Anna and Emma loved that. That night though, "Rocky the Cat" banged into Emma and knocked her to the ground. Naturally, Rocky was speechless. He/she/it held its hand (paw) over its mouth, over its heart, then wiped away imaginary tears. Before long, Rocky disappeared once it recognized Emma was okay. A few minutes later, a strange man arrived and presented Emma with a mascot-autographed T-shirt. Who was this dude? How did he know about this? When you're tired, sometimes you miss the obvious.

PRIDE AT THE DUQUESNE INCLINE

I took the kids to the Duquesne Incline in Pittsburgh a few years ago. When you visit there, one parking option is to pay with a credit card and leave your vehicle at the bottom of the hill, across the street. That is what we did. No problem. You put in your parking spot number, insert the card, and are done. Then to get to the Incline itself, you need to climb the many stairs and cross the catwalk that goes over the street. We did all of that. Upon entering the base building, where you board the Incline ride itself, there was a short line. We waited, of course. Finally, upon getting to the ticket booth, we learned the ride is cash only! "Johnny don't carry cash anymore," I often tell the kids.

Time out, readers! There is nothing abnormal about any of this. I am not alone in not carrying cash though I know I probably should always try to have a little on hand—you know, "just in case." But I don't. I try to travel lightly. Call me foolish, whatever. Now while I am being read the house rules by the woman working there, the base incline building was loaded with people, but it was pretty quiet, and all of the tourists waiting to board the next car up were sitting in a formation that had them staring at me, listening. If Johnny don't carry cash, Johnny really don't like being embarrassed in public. So in typical "Johnny mode," I tell the kids, "let's go! They don't take cards. We gotta go!"

I try to leave and head back to the catwalk en route to the car. Of course, my kids, being more rational than I am and wondering if there are any alternatives (wise of them—that is the appropriate response in this situation; I am aware of that), start conversing with the woman who sells the tickets. As I am trying to lead my flock back and realizing I am halfway across the said catwalk and no one else is leaving the building, I hear: "Dad, come back! Dad!" Then even the lady starts in, "Sir? Sir?" Again, Johnny don't play these games. Once Johnny is embarrassed, Johnny is out of there—at all costs! My kids just had not yet learned the severity of Dad's pride issue until they got to the Duquesne Incline, of all places.

I waited silently in the catwalk. Once Emma poked around the corner and saw me, I shot her "the look." She knew! There was no alternative! That lady could yell "sir" all day long. Johnny ain't responding! Emma passed the word to Anna and Joey. Before long, the four of us were outta there!

We went to a local gas station. I paid a $3 service fee to take out cash from the ATM, and we went back to the Incline. I repaid to park, and we enjoyed the beautiful view of the city from the top of the hill via the cash-only ride. This was all okay as that initial group, who saw my fallacy, had moved along by this point. And that's how I roll.

A REFLECTION THAT IS LONG OVERDUE

There's a ton written about the men and women of our United States military who sacrifice their time, innocence, and sometimes their lives in the name of serving our homeland. Today, I listened to a mix of songs, and Guns N Roses' rendition of "Knockin' on Heaven's Door" came on. Immediately, like so many pieces do, it threw me into a particular place and time. When we deployed to Iraq for our first deployment in March 2003, I had a couple of CDs (compact discs, a music source in between cassette tapes and Spotify) given to me. One was from my buddy from high school, Matt Meyer, and another was from my brother-in-law, Tim. I don't remember whose burnt CD included Axl's version of the Dylan classic, but I would often listen to that quite a bit in the weeks before the war kicked off but while we were still in our Kuwaiti "holding cell." We knew we were headed north to Iraq just as soon as the war started. But for a handful of days and nights when our work was done, I would lay in a bunk in a warehouse-like facility (with near five hundred other soldiers joining me), pop my headphones in, and listen. Same two or three CDs, over and over. It was all I had.

I got to thinking, *Knocking on heaven's door?* Is that what they (Matt and/or Tim) imagined was happening to us? Was this some kind of subliminal message? AC/DC's "Highway to Hell" also made the mix, I recall. Queen's "Under Pressure" too. All ended up being so appropriate. In fact, now when I hear those particular songs, I immediately and only think of Iraq, April 2003. But after much reflection in the past pandemic-ridden year, I have this to say: We got deployed in 2003. (After the events of September 11, 2001, it was kind of a big deal nationally.) Then shortly after we came home, we found ourselves right back in Iraq in 2005 and did not get home from that second tour until late 2006. I had gotten married between the two deployments, and my wife became pregnant shortly after our '06 homecoming. Then we had twins in 2007, and that life swept us up. I had a relatively new career that required going back to school to earn my MSW and my social work license. In 2010, we had our son. We were busy, with our hands full. Three years later, we moved to the Midwest for a career opportunity that seemed to make sense for everyone, all things considered. Before I knew it, our first deployment was seventeen years in the rearview mirror, and I had not even checked that reflection. Seventeen years! To me, it seemed like seventeen months. All this time rolled by, and I had not really stopped to think about a huge factor: the friends and families and neighbors of those of us who went off to war—or twice to the same war. Holy cow! I can't stand seeing my kids near the edge of a tall building when we're on an observation deck. I get worried when my now-teen daughters walk by themselves to Dunkin' Donuts down the street. I don't like when my son is home too late and I know he is alone on his bike.

How did you all do it? How did you rest? You must have been worried sick! I know I would have been. You saw grisly news accounts. You saw names coming across the TV. You heard the news and only got vague messages that said five US troops were killed this morning, or six marines have perished overnight, or we lost twenty soldiers in an Iraqi ambush. You didn't know who those people were. You had no idea. You had to go about your day. How did you do it? How did you stay focused on your jobs? How did you not get so depressed? Did you? My goodness. You probably did! How could you not? And no one recognizes the extreme bravery you had to produce to handle that shit. Wow. I am sorry. I never stopped to think too deeply about it or to acknowledge your experience(s). Having been there and back, I honestly think it might be scarier to be on this side and have no idea what is happening there instead of the other way around. At least when you're there, granted, there are present dangers abound, but you have a finger on the pulse of the activity. But at home, pure blindness. You have totally no idea, and for so long, sometimes more than once (or twice or more)! Goodness! I want you to know I appreciate that kind of bravery—it might be the most incredible kind there is! It's time you receive your due credit! I wish I could be as brave as you were! Truly! Thank you for the music. It did calm my nerves when I needed it most!

EMPIRE STATE BUILDING ANALOGY

One hundred people sign up for a chance to make some money and volunteer to take part in an expedition. The one hundred volunteers get to know each other, become friends, and even develop strong relationships throughout a short period.

Once the trial begins though, they are brought to the 102nd story of the Empire State Building—the outside observation deck—above Midtown Manhattan. The group is divided into four sections, each with twenty-five people. One team is chosen to go to the east-facing platform, one to the north, one to the south, and one to the west.

The trial shall only take a few moments. The volunteers stand shoulder to shoulder and face outward on the very edge of the building overlooking the busy city. They are given just a few simple rules: one person from each side will be tapped on the shoulder. Once that person is chosen, they shall step backward, off the edge, and return to the platform (to safety). The remaining twenty-four volunteers (on each side of the observatory), who were not selected with a tap, are to continue standing on the edge until they are pushed off, or they witness or hear another volunteer being pushed to their certain death. Once one person from each side has perished, specifically by the person who had been tapped on the shoulder, the twenty-three survivors on each side shall step down, and the trial is complete.

During the immediate after-action review, ninety-six volunteers gather inside the observation deck's interior conference room. Four of their friends are dead. Four of the volunteers are responsible for having pushed another human being to his/her death. Ninety-two people did not die and did not directly take anyone's life—they just stood on the observation deck, much like hundreds of tourists have done.

Question: How many of the volunteers will be affected by this experience?

(This story was developed considering the effect of going to combat has on people—regardless of job, mission, branch, location, rank, gender, etc. No one knows if they will survive. No one knows if they will take another's life. No one knows if they will see their friend perish. There does not always need to be a specific "story" for someone to experience trauma.)

Jay and Jessica White

COVERT-19 GEN X AND SOCIAL MEDIA

The Internet and social media are exciting concepts, especially for those of us from Generation X. Gone are the days of "dropping a dime to stop a crime." Gone is carrying a map and asking for directions, looking up books with the Dewey Decimal system at the local library, writing a paper with a typewriter, and getting up to change the channel on your TV. No more Blockbuster video. No more rabbit ears. No more Rolodex. Hardly a need to carry a wallet. Almost no more paper money. Stamps, envelopes, the daily paper, even taxi cabs—they are all hanging on by a thread. Want ads and transferable plane tickets, gone. Tickets in general? Better have an iPhone and scanner (well, that was back when you could go out in public). Doghouses, stray cats, cigarettes at a restaurant, and helmet-less bicyclists, all yesteryear.

We did our thing in the '70s, '80s, and '90s. We worked hard, played hard, had fun, tried to stay in line, and eventually had to choose a direction or go in the direction life put us in as time moved on. Things changed in the first thirty years of the Gen Xers' lives, but not like they changed after September 11, coupled with the birth and growth of the Internet and then the boom of social media. Frankly, as someone who lived on both sides of this bridge, I don't really know if we were prepared for the speed of this change. If you were born into this concept, it might be second nature to have an app for this, an app for that, Uber here, Uber there, TikTok, Twitter, hashtag Zoom, Hulu, lama dama ding dong. But holy shit. This is a complete mind twister if you take any time to reflect back and think of how much things have been contorted.

For many years, I did not get to go back to see old friends, be it the army, college, life in general. There was a time that I had all but accepted that I may never see old friends again. I would most certainly have no idea about their lives, how they grew into adulthood, what kind of perspective they took on our world, how they found their niches, the obstacles they encountered, who they fell in love with, or what they enjoyed to do. I never loved computers or technology. I was the one who did not care to play video games and only got cable when school was out in the summer. I was one of the last to get an email address, and I still use my original Hotmail account. I didn't use Myspace and only dabbled on Facebook at first as the fear of losing privacy seemed like it might jeopardize my work as a counselor. So I stayed away. But so did friends and then even family. Of course, I had kids, which is a natural distractor, but once they started growing up and I had more of a chance to look around a bit again, I realized I had put isolation and social distancing in fashion years before any pandemic. I was COVERT-19.

Slowly, I reentered the social media realm. The choice felt inevitable, though I resisted for some reason. There is a lot of stress with social media. It's a political echo chamber. Lots of friends on the left and far left. Lots of friends on the right. Wear masks! Don't wear masks! Biden! Trump! Stay the blank home! "I only love my cat!" Look what we made for dinner! Tom Brady is the GOAT! "When we were kids…and it shows!" On and on. Mindless at times. So I focused on baseball groups, Patriots groups, funny videos, and catching up with old chums, slowly but surely, if only adding or requesting them as "friends" (again? still?).

"Hey, friend, wanna be my friend?" Twenty years ago, I (and many of you, I imagine) would have thought this ludicrous. But here we are. Now I stay in touch with my high school baseball teammates, coworkers, old neighbors, current neighbors, my third-grade teacher, battle buddies, fellow veterans, cousins, aunts, uncles, nephews, and in-laws. I read about activities they do daily. It is comforting—like a resurrection of sorts. To see faces of decades past emerge in the current—whoa! I did not see this coming. But here it is.

For all it is and has become, I will share that this past week, my month was made when I got on the phone and shared two to three hours of laughing and reminiscing with a kid I met in second grade.

Mike and I reconstructed our pasts and determined that we moved to Maine in 1978 and joined Mrs. Johnson's class at Ogunquit Village School. We dug up old names. We stoked each other's memories. Mike and I might have had more in common when we were young than we had ever known and needed to become adults to discover that. We both had to leave the small town and find our own path. We both admit to being young at heart and tirelessly seeking to learn, unearth and explore the world, even as we move into our fifties. After I had set out, I did not fathom this day would ever happen. I thought Mike Nadeau was a great kid, but over time figured he was a kid I would probably never hear from again. But he remembered me, and I remembered him. We placed a lot of the same events and, of course, the same people. We played in the same Little League and did Cub Scouts together. We were in the same classes in elementary school, junior high school, and freshman year of high school. When he reminded me of a specific time at recess, it was heartwarming to know that we could both recall the exact same bike rack and exact same swing set. I thought this time was sealed only in my own head. There is another person who shares that location, those times, and memories with me…years after I had thought that impossible to discover? My goodness. I am beyond moved—I am taken aback!

VETERANS DAY

In Washington, the Vietnam Memorial had been built just a few years prior when our family stopped to pay a visit on our drive back to Maine from Florida during April vacation in 1985. My father had been drafted and served in Vietnam in the late '60s, but I was not too sure of his roles, experiences, or history there—it almost seemed like that had never happened based on the number of times it came up in conversation over the years. Sure, there was a Fort Dix Basic Training picture book on a shelf, and I liked to get into his Class A suit when I was young, but other than our dad having lost a good amount of his hearing, and much that was said had to be repeated at least once, Vietnam was not the focal point—to us.

I am not sure what struck Dad that day in DC. Not only did I not dare ask but I was absolutely frozen in the moment of seeing him appear to be crying. Dad? Crying? Never before! What happened? Why? What made you cry? Of course, these were only my thoughts—no way did I verbalize this. I could not help him. I wanted to, but I was too stunned! I remember the day so well that I believe I could go to the Memorial today and draw a circle around the exact spot where Dad was standing when this happened thirty-five years ago.

That day, as a fourteen-year-old boy, I thought, *The people who are memorialized on the wall don't have it as hard as the service members whose names will never be put on there.* Of course, those who gave their lives in Vietnam (and any event) are sorely missed and the loss grievous. They are heroic! But I went on thinking, *Their suffering is over. They are not injured. They are not deaf. They are not sad. They do not get angry. They are still nineteen and should be in a muscle car or at a beach or somewhere in Florida or New Jersey or Texas.* But to survive and have to deal with the aftereffects and never get due credit—that may be worse!

Of course, I was only fourteen. Thank God my father did survive. I will never know how he has handled himself so well over the years. He is why I try to understand and help veterans every day.

8.0 IN PERU

On Saturday, May 25, 2019, I traveled to Lima, Peru, with two Edgewood College classmates and our professor to begin a two-week course that would conclude our international sustainability course, semester, and, ultimately, my school-bound academic life. We landed in the Pacific nation's capital that evening (Peru and Wisconsin are in the same time zone). We got a taxi and made our way through the city to our hotel. After checking in, we all made our separate ways to our rooms.

I marveled at the fabulous balcony attached to my room, with the more astonishing architecture visible in the courtyard enveloping the area. The windows in the room and the bathroom were unique. I had not seen anything quite like them. The way they maneuvered was much different from anything I had been used to, but I propped them open to let some fresh air. Finally, I went to bed. A couple hours later, my room started gyrating. *Oh no. Did I leave that sliding door open? What was I thinking*? I looked up and saw that it was closed. The gyrating feeling continued. *What the hell is happening?* Now my thoughts are getting more serious. My bed would not stop shaking. It was like my room was a plane hitting heavy turbulence. That's what it felt like: sustained heavy turbulence, only in my bed. I texted my professor, Steve, for no other reason than to mark time. The shaking seemed to last one to two minutes—quite a while for an unknown invader to wake you up and jostle you around. It got me all fired up, of course. I didn't want to call home and scare anyone.

I googled "Peru earthquake" or something like that. Nothing. I kept googling it, pretty convinced that that is what that had to have been. Probably about 3:00 AM, BBC reported that, indeed, Peru had just experienced an earthquake. Apparently, its center was somewhere north and east of us, in the Amazon jungle portion of Peru. But it turned out to be the largest earthquake in the world (based on magnitude) in all of 2019 and the largest earthquake (also based solely on Richter scale measurements) ever recorded in Peru. We hadn't even seen sunlight there yet.

KNOTICAL

A little boat would charter small groups of people for a full or half day of deep-sea fishing trips off the coast of Maine. It docked at a local cove and, during the deepest summer weeks, would make two trips each day. Earlier in the season, it was not uncommon to just make one trip. Instead, it stayed out on the water for the entire day (no return to the cove), weather permitting, of course.

One day in early May, when one of these full-day trips was scheduled, the first mate called in sick, leaving only me to handle a full roster of firefighters, who had flown up from New Jersey for the day, to get out on the ocean—me and the owner, who was the captain of the boat, that is. The captain was a cranky old guy who struggled to get around on a weak old pair of sore knees. His attitude matched his ortho pain. He was no fun to be around, and I didn't know it would be just me alone with him all day until I arrived at the dock just after 5:00 AM. When he saw me, he gave me that snarly look he would often throw out there. Being in my early twenties and having no defense for such an attitude developed yet, I just dealt with him.

Before we shoved off though, he took me to the side of the boat, on the dock, and demonstrated how I should be tying the boat down when we were to return at the end of the day. The knots did not look to be rocket science, but his poor teaching skill and nasty behavior, all the while with a dozen excited firefighters looking on just feet away, made it damn near impossible for me to match his rope-tying skills. Immediately, he had wanted me to prove that I had learned what he had just shown me. Of course, my knots were not up to his snuff at first blush, and he had about as much patience as he had running speed. He started swearing and yelling. He really humiliated me in front of this gang with whom I needed to work all day, and I was his only help.

He is long gone now, but it was only a few years ago that I stopped regretting not having walked away from the bastard and leaving him in a lurch—where he deserved to be that day. When my superiors have questioned why I am kind or friendly or compassionate to people who may work for me or who have been a lower rank than me, I tell them it should not be any other way.

36X34

I was invited to come to the Hartford Armory to join a board to discuss veteran issues and soldier transitions. I figured that would be a good day to break out my new dress slacks. Luckily, the only parking was a reasonable distance from the building because that forced me to cross Capitol Ave. At the corner, waiting for the light, I swiped my right hand past the back of my leg and felt something odd. This is what I found:

36x34
36x34
36x34
36x34
36x34
36x34
36x34
36x34
36x34
36x34

S'MORE HITTIN'

When I was a kid, we played Wiffle ball.
I would shove Jet-Puffed marshmallows into the side of my mouth.
I wanted to look like Wade Boggs, and I think I pulled it off.
Our similarities ended there.

PORT STANLEY, ONTARIO

Lake Erie's gem.
Blue water. Yellow perch.
King George VI welcomes us there.
The old green train greets us.
The cottages. The quiet. The maple leaf flag.
Mackies' fries and orangeade by day.
Cold Labatts, a grill, and music at night.
Breathtaking vistas display distant lightning when all are asleep.
A storied history.
A great getaway.
A lifetime of memories.
Family and friends from the Forest City visit us.
Rosalee. Orvilla. Buttonwood.
You've all lent your space
The high sky and youthful exuberance.
Port Stanley shines in my heart.

THE STAR OF HACKMATACK

At the Hackmatack Playhouse in Berwick, Maine, we took in a show called *Run for Your Wife*. Hackmatack is a local, almost-barn-like, summer stage venue that provides quality live theater to the non-oceanfront parts of southernmost Maine. Our seats in the old wooden structure were terrific and gave us a great vantage point of the activity.

On this night, one of the female actors tripped on the set's living room carpet and fell very hard into its coffee table. Clearly, she hit her face on the corner of the furniture. The sound was shocking. At first glance, I don't think anyone was sure whether or not her gaffe was real or "part of the script." Immediately though, her cheek visibly began to swell, and it looked like she wanted to cry. But she never stopped to acknowledge the fall, which bolstered the thought that was not an intentional move. After that, her ability to maintain focus was one of the most impressive performances I have ever seen—sports, theater, you name it. She received a much-deserved rousing standing ovation during the final bow.

THE GREAT(ER) NEELY

I used to tell my buddies at school in Florida about the greatness of professional ice hockey. One of my favorite stories to share with them was one that I had seen live on television. I would demonstrate the scene: I stood up and pretended to be the Boston Bruins star Cam Neely, picking up a defenseless and much weaker Claude Lemieux. I/Neely would air-pound Lemieux until he dropped, then pick Lemieux up by the back of his Devils' sweater, and continue the pounding until he could no longer take it. Then finally, I showed them how Neely ended the brouhaha by sliding Lemieux headfirst into the Boston Garden boards. I painted Cam Neely into the hero role for sticking up for teammate Ray Bourque, who I would explain had just been cross-checked by Lemieux in front of the net.

The NHL had yet to be born in Florida at that point, and the local Tampa Bay Lightning were already a good ten to fifteen years old by the time YouTube became a household name. So many years later, I have pulled up the video of that fight. It does not necessarily match my story. I mean, kinda, but not really. Not all the way through. Holy moly. What other stories have I told that don't match reality? I added serious customized touch-up paint to the actual event. Oh well! So one time, the Patriots were down 28-3 with just over seventeen minutes left in the Super Bowl…

FANTASTIC FIFTY

I will be a half-century old on May 29. Part of me thinks, *Oh my, I am getting up there. I am definitely entering the absolute prime time of the creepy old man age range!* Then I think: *How am I only fifty? It seems like I have been around forever. Just fifty?* As I inch toward the years that, when listed in an obituary, people stop thinking *What happened?* and shift to, *Well, a life well-lived,* I feel overly reflective right now.

Of course, like many things, and I suppose like many people, I tend to remember most of the good events when I am looking back, and definitely when I choose which stories or memories to share publicly, something that I have enjoyed doing this past year. But truth be told, life is not always so easy. There has been a good amount of discomfort or frustration trying to figure out who I am and how I fit in, now and over the years. If you had asked me when I was eighteen if I imagined that I would have been "all set" (meaning me being comfortable with who I am, that is) by the time I was turning fifty, I think I would have given you a resounding yes! But in reality, the answer is still similar (if not less of yes) to when I was eighteen. Maybe I am no closer to answering the BIG question (Who am I?), but I think my approach to it has grown and changed, and it was not possible to view it as I do now from when I was only eighteen or even thirty-five.

In fact, just yesterday, I had a great phone conversation with one of my closest friends, who is a decade behind me age-wise but a decade ahead of me maturity-wise and who mentioned that he was facing a similar self-challenge. I told him, "I think I might go to my grave not fully knowing who I am!" I have frequently discussed this topic, especially with another close friend and coworker in my same age bracket. I know this whole idea may sound unsettling, and it kind of is, but I think once I embraced it, it made life lighter and more enjoyable, quite frankly (at least for me).

I share this because I think and talk about this idea a lot, and I am not so certain that many men, especially, speak like this with other men. I think men battle with the concept of figuring out who they are in life and may not realize so many other men do too. Perhaps they would be better off discussing it more and recognizing it is not just a battle of theirs and then learning to embrace that discomfort. Imagine? We're supposed to tell an interviewer where we "see ourselves in five years" when often, the truth is we don't even actually know who the blank we are (and neither does the interviewer) now still!

In fifty years, there have been so many things I have gotten to do. Many life events grow in importance as I recognize that time cannot replace them, and I am grateful that they happened. I met all four of my grandparents and my great-grandmother, all of whom have since passed. I have planned a get-together for May 29, 2021, and both of my parents plan to be there together. I know how fortunate I am to say that. I got to go to work with my father. I listened to Seals & Crofts on his eight-track. I had a mother who sacrificed a career to be home with us every day and who was our number one advocate. I have three sisters and enjoyed my time with them growing up. I got to go to college and live to see the day I paid that off. I got to get two master's degrees, both of which were covered through my military service. How cool!

I have snuck into two World Series games, worked at a Super Bowl game, and run a dozen marathons. I have been in person to see Michael Jordan dunk a basketball, Tom Brady throw a touchdown, and watched Wayne Gretzky play in his prime (no goal, but two assists). I pitched two innings at Fenway Park. I got the courage to ask the girl I most had a crush on in junior high school to dance with me (thank you for saying yes!). I visited all of the Great Lakes. I pulled off a prank on a national TV news piece. I encouraged an injured man in a car accident to hang in there until help came. I gave my buddy the Heimlich in the college cafeteria. I cofounded a sports talk show for local cable TV. I got to volunteer as a Big Brother and teach English in Korea.

I sprained my ankle at the actual shortstop location of the Field of Dreams field in Iowa. I graduated from professional umpire school. I remember exactly where I was when Thurman Munson, Princess Diana, Christa McAuliffe, Michael Jackson, and Lenny Bias all perished. I busted my arm so badly that the fire department had to be called to help me to the ambulance. I survived Iraq a couple of times and met some of the most loyal and trusting people ever in that experience. I stayed up all night when my Red Sox won the World Series in 2004 and walked across Boston to greet the team bus as it arrived at Fenway at 7:00 AM. I got to thank Paul Simon for all his great years of musical contribution—with a handshake—and I got Springsteen's attention when I yelled out "Bruuuuce" as he drove by us en route to his stage in Boston (he nodded acceptingly at me). I have been honored and blessed to work with veterans—to advocate and support them as they leave behind the military and adjust to civilian life. In fact, I suggest that my experience with veterans for nearly eighteen years now has allowed me to be more open, candid, and brave in having these sorts of discussions.

Most importantly, I have been able to watch three children be born and then rely on me. That has been the biggest eye-opener (and challenge). I often doubt myself. We have had our share of struggles, and this COVID-19 isolation has heightened a lot of that. But they have given me a tremendous sense of purpose, and without them, I am not sure where I would be (let alone who I am—oh, goodness)!

The only goal I made up before turning fifty is to submit all of these stories in a compilation to a publisher. I did not intend to do that initially, but many of you have given me positive feedback with some of these stories I have shared, and recommended that I author something. I am all about ripping off the Band-Aid (though I still look over the proverbial edge of many things and tend to hem and haw with shaky knees). I have googled something like, "What is the word count of a published book?" In my mind, I set out to get at least fifty thousand words done. Before this actual writing, I had 49,252 counted. Right now, this alone is at 971, putting me into my target range of feeling adequate submitting this all to a publisher. If I complete my preface piece this week, I am going to send in a manuscript. We'll see what happens.

I am fifty years old. I still have no idea what I want to do when I grow up. I still like watching Christmas specials and get goose bumps when I rewatch the 1980 US Olympic hockey team or Live Aid on YouTube. I am sure that I would feel as shy now as I did when I was thirteen years old if I were to see the girl I had a crush on in junior high school. I hung up my baseball spikes just a year or two ago because my inability to regularly throw strikes led to too much anxiety. I worry that I cannot continue working as much as I do and may fail to provide for my family. I have gray hair now—and not too much of it. My triceps and quads are not as big as they had been. I sit at work too much. I have a mortgage that is so far from being paid off I barely want to open the envelope when the weekly (oh, is that monthly?) bill comes in. I appreciate hearing that the "dad bod" is a thing to admire (sweet!). I listen to '80s music. I worry about my children's future. But, I have learned that life is pretty fast. There is a lot out there. My perspective is just my perspective. I need to listen to others more. I need to strive to better understand their perspective and to continue to work on myself. I have a lot to do in that arena.

I am learning that I need not worry about who I am, per se. Instead, I believe what is essential is discovering what I have to contribute. That is all. How can I use any of my strengths to be of assistance to you or anyone else? That's all this is about, I have gathered. You can have the big quads and triceps. You can have the tight slider I used to be able to throw. You can have marathons. You can have the greenest lawn and the fastest car. You can have the Curse of the Bambino. I like being at this stage of life. It is my time to share. It's pretty human to struggle, and I think we all need to be freer to admit that. How could we not struggle? We need to laugh more. We're just human! On to the other side of life's bell curve. Go, Pats.

ABOUT THE AUTHOR

Please enjoy Jay's first book. He hopes this is his "rookie card" as he hopes to produce many more. Jay has spent the last eighteen years working with veterans and is a social worker. He served in the Army Reserves and did two deployments to Iraq. He has also held over forty jobs—from being a ball boy for the Red Sox to a street messenger in New York City—which have afforded him all sorts of interesting experiences. He turned fifty this year and wanted the name of this book to be a tip of the cap to the town where it all started for him: Brockton, Massachusetts. Jay is a recently retired men's league baseball (not softball!) pitcher. He is now building a private practice that will allow him to focus on his real passion: men's wellness. He lives in Wisconsin with his family.

CPSIA information can be obtained
at www.ICGtesting.com
Printed in the USA
LVHW010128190422
716592LV00006B/116

9 781638 609520